Start Reading for Adults
M.C. Vincent

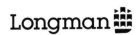

Longman Group Limited,
Longman House, Burnt Mill, Harlow,
Essex CM20 2JE, England
Associated Companies throughout the world.

© Longman Group Limited 1984
All rights reserved; no part of this publication
may be reproduced, stored in a retrieval system
or transmitted in any form or by any means, electronic,
mechanical, photocopying, recording, or otherwise,
without the prior written permission of the Publishers.

First published 1984
Second impression 1986
ISBN 0 582 52637 X

Set in 11/13pt Monophoto Plantin 110
Produced by Longman Group (FE) Ltd
Printed in Hong Kong

Contents

To the teacher

Start Reading for Adults is a collection of original articles designed to develop the understanding of written English as a means of communication. The topics relate to the content areas in course books for beginners and elementary students, and to the wide range of interests of adult learners. The texts exemplify the main functions of written language: narration, description, exposition, instruction, argument and persuasion, while the style varies from the formal to the colloquial and the tone from the serious to the humorous.

The language has been controlled to make it easily accessible to learners in their first or second year of English and the texts are structurally and lexically graded as follows:

Units 1–4   Longman Structural Readers Level 2
Units 5–9   Longman Structural Readers Level 3
Units 10–15 Longman Structural Readers Level 4

In addition, subject-specific vocabulary has been introduced throughout.

The exercises at the end of each unit provide material for pre-reading, while-reading and post-reading activities, and, like the texts, they gradually become more difficult and demanding. It is therefore advisable to work through the units in numerical order. Otherwise a flexible approach to teaching procedures based on your students' needs and interests is recommended.

Start Reading for Adults can be used in several ways:

1 As a first intensive course in how to read a foreign language, with the focus on reading styles and strategies and learning language *for* reading.
2 As a supplement to the general course book, providing more exposure to English in class and a stimulus for related language activities. Here the focus is on intensive, integrated reading and learning language *from* reading.
3 As material to encourage individual private reading out of class, with the focus on extensive reading at the students' own pace and in their own time.

The following suggestions are for using the book in class.

Learning to read

1 Preparation

It often helps students learning to read a foreign language if you prepare them for the text by introducing the topic and a few key language items in advance. The first exercise, *Before you read*, suggests various approaches to text preparation: activating knowledge the students already possess or raising questions to which the text will provide an answer, surveying the illustrations to get a general idea of the content or studying a related piece of information to focus their minds on the topic of the text.

The teacher is the best person to decide what vocabulary is difficult or unfamiliar, but only pre-teach words that are (a) essential for understanding the main ideas of the text and (b) cannot be deduced from the context. Remember, the preparation stage is just a warm-up for tackling the text, not a substitute for reading it.

2 First main reading

(a) Tell the students to read each article through without stopping and without worrying about every single word. Remind them to look at the illustrations and captions while they read, as this helps make the meaning of important words and concepts clear. On no account ask or allow the students to read the texts aloud in class, but emphasise the importance of silent reading for ideas and information.

(b) Ask the students to try the first general comprehension exercise, *Read for ideas*, *Read for main points*, *Read for reasons*. Do not expect them to do these exercises from memory, but always with their books open so they can refer to the text. Then go over the answers.

Variations

– If you read the text aloud while your students follow in their books this will help them to read through the texts at a steady pace.
– If this is your students' first experience of reading longer texts you can break the first

reading and comprehension check into sections, following the natural breaks in the units. Then tell the students to read through the whole text again silently.

– You can help focus your students' attention on the main points by going through the questions in *Read for ideas* before they start the text.

3 Second Main Reading

(a) Prepare the students for more detailed reading by reminding them how to tackle new words. The following checklist uses examples from Unit 1 to demonstrate some basic strategies.

1 Look for illustrations of words. *Example:* a bracelet

2 Look for a definition in the text. *Example:* 'A *voice synthesiser* can make the sounds of human speech.'

3 Look for exemplification of meaning in the context. *Example:* 'You – dirty – bad – toilet' exemplifies 'rude', 'rudely'.

4 Try to work out the meaning of the word from the wider context of the whole passage. *Example:* 'clever' can be deduced from all the things Koko can do.

5 Look for international words or words similar to those in the first language. *Examples:* Africa, machine.

In many units there will be a small residue of words that students cannot work out for themselves and which cannot easily be explained in simple English or by devices such as demonstration. The most effective way to deal with words such as 'strange' is for the teacher to provide a quick translation or to refer students to personal bilingual dictionaries. Do not translate the whole text or ask your students to do so, as this will defeat the purpose of this book: to encourage students to read English in a manner as close as possible to that in which they read their own language.

(b) Tell the students to read the text again in order to answer the questions in the second group of exercises: *Read for detail*, *Read for inference*, *Check the facts*. These exercises provide practice in scanning – looking for specific information, and train the students to relate one part of the text to another, or to read between the lines. They also encourage the reader to interpret and integrate information presented in different formats and introduce some basic note-making techniques. In going over these exercises stress the importance of varying the style of reading to suit different purposes.

Variations

– Students can work in pairs or small groups. Remind them that they should always justify their answers by reference to the text.

– Set the exercises for homework and go over them in class.

Learning from Reading

When the students are fully familiar with the content of the units they are ready for follow-up exercises. These fall into two broad categories: (a) read for response and (b) read for language. The exercises *What do you think?* or *Talk about . . .* encourage students to respond to what they have read by drawing on their own knowledge and experience, and are best suited for small group work followed by class discussion. Most students should be able to express their ideas orally in simple English, but if this proves too difficult or frustrating allow the use of the mother tongue for this activity.

The section *Read for language* focuses on the vocabulary, structure and main communicative functions of written English, and can be set as homework. The vocabulary exercises give practice in classifying and defining words, understanding idiom, and grasping the principles of word formation in English. Structural points which occur in the text or arise naturally from the topic are practised through sentence-building exercises, and the section ends with more open-ended work concentrating on using the text as a model or stimulus for communicative writing.

Finally each unit ends with a light-hearted text, quiz or task which gives students a further opportunity to respond to written English with ease and enjoyment and the confidence to go on reading English for information, interest and pleasure.

1 CAN KOKO TALK?

Gorillas come from Africa, but this gorilla lives in America. Her name is Koko, and she is eleven years old. Other gorillas live in zoos, but Koko lives with Penny Patterson, an American psychologist. Penny is teaching Koko a special language, *Ameslan* or American Sign Language. *Ameslan* is the language of deaf people in America, and in other countries too. Deaf people cannot hear, so they often do not learn to speak well. Their voices are strange, and other people cannot understand them easily. With *Ameslan* deaf people do not have to speak. *Ameslan* is a language of signs, not words. So deaf people learn to talk with their hands. They make special signs and these signs mean words or ideas.

Gorillas can hear very well, but they cannot learn to speak. Their mouths and tongues are different from human ones, so they cannot make the sounds of speech. But Koko is learning to talk, with signs. She uses *Ameslan*. Penny first taught her gorilla the signs for 'food', 'drink' and 'more'. So Koko quickly learned to ask for food and drink. With signs she could soon say, 'I am hungry' or 'I want a drink.' Now Koko knows 400 signs and talks to Penny all the time.

Penny has a lot of friends and visitors. Koko talks to them too. She shows them her room and she talks about their clothes. She asks them, 'Do you want a drink?' or 'Have you brought some fruit for me?' On warm days Penny takes Koko out for a walk. Koko likes ball games, but she always wants to have the ball. One day a visitor took the ball and ran across the grass. Koko ran after him and bit him. Penny was very angry. 'Why did you do that?' she asked. Koko answered, 'Him – ball – bad.'

But is Koko really talking to Penny? Is she really using language? Some birds can learn to repeat words, but they do not understand them. Is Koko just repeating the signs? Or does she understand them too? Penny says, 'Koko really does understand the signs, so she *is* using human language. She is learning our language and she can use it in new ways. I have not taught her all her signs. She thinks of new ones without any help from me. She has her own sign for "ring". She calls it a "finger bracelet". Koko put the two signs for "finger" and "bracelet" together and made one new

food

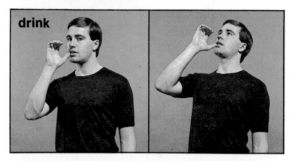

drink

more

Koko is talking to Penny in sign language. Penny's sign means "How?" ('How are you?'). Koko's sign means 'Good' ('I'm well').

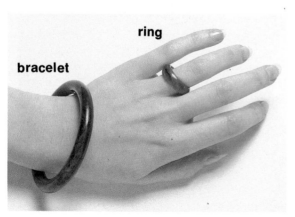

ring

bracelet

sign. Koko does not just repeat old signs. And another thing, she can talk about yesterday and tomorrow. She uses signs for "sad" or "happy" at the right time too. This is really using sign language, and understanding it.'

Koko tells lies as well. One day she took a stick and tried to make a hole through the window. But Penny came in and saw her. Koko quickly put the stick in her mouth, but Penny took it from her.

'What are you doing, Koko?' she asked.

Koko answered with two signs. The first one meant 'smoke'. The second one meant 'mouth'. So Koko said, 'I am smoking,' or 'The stick is my cigarette.' This was a lie, and both Penny and Koko knew it.

Koko often plays with Penny's friend, Eugene, but one day she suddenly bit him.

'What did you do?' asked Penny.

'Not teeth,' said Koko.

'Koko, you lied!'

'Bad – again – Koko – bad – again,' said the unhappy gorilla.

'Koko can tell lies,' says Penny, 'so Koko really understands language.'

Koko has already learned to be rude. One day Penny found two legs from Koko's doll. 'Koko pulled them off,' she thought, but Penny was wrong. It was her other gorilla, Michael. 'You bad girl,' Penny said to Koko, 'You have broken your doll. You pulled its legs off.' Koko was very angry, and said to Penny, 'I didn't do it. It was Michael.' And then she said, very rudely, 'You – dirty – bad – toilet.'

Koko likes picture books, and often talks about the pictures. In this photo Penny is telling Koko the story of three little kittens. 'They lost their mittens,' she reads. Koko is making the sign for 'angry'. Another time Koko saw a picture of an animal with very big eyes. She made the sign for 'eye'. So Koko can talk about pictures. And she is beginning to read words too.

Penny is now teaching Koko to speak, through machines: a computer and a voice synthesiser. A voice synthesiser can make the sounds of human speech. Koko presses a key on the computer keyboard and the voice

computer with voice synthesiser

2 The voice synthesiser makes the sound

keyboard

3 Koko hears the sound

1 Koko presses the keys

loudspeaker

synthesiser makes the right sounds. Then Koko hears the sound of the word through a loudspeaker. In the photo on page 9 Penny is asking Koko, 'Shall I make you a drink?' Koko presses the keys for 'want – milk – drink – want.' Then she hears these words from the loudspeaker. Penny first uses the sign and the word together. Then she uses the word only. She is trying to teach Koko to use words. Koko must learn to listen to the sound of words. Then she has to answer with words –

from her special machines.

So, can Koko use human language, or is she just a very clever animal? Koko understands Penny, but dogs and cats often understand human speech. But dogs cannot use *Ameslan*. Cats do not talk through a computer. People are different from animals, we say. People can speak, but animals cannot. People have language, but animals do not. What about Koko? Can she really use language? Can Koko talk? What do you think?

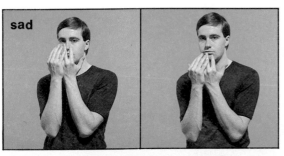

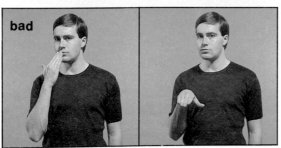

Notes
kitten young cat.
mittens small children wear mittens on their hands.

10

Exercises

A Before you read
1 Look at the signs on p. 10. Where do they come from? Who uses them? Can you say, 'I'm happy', or 'He's sad', in sign language?

2 What can animals do? Put **YES, NO** or **?** in the right column.

	Dogs	Cats	Koko
can ask for food			
can understand speech			
can play games			
can repeat words			
can understand signs			
can make signs			
can talk about tomorrow			
can tell lies			
can talk about pictures			
can use machines			

B Read for ideas
1 What can Koko the gorilla do? Put **YES, NO** or **?** in the column above for Koko.

2 Koko does a lot of clever things. She does bad things too. Find three examples.

3 Tell Koko's story. Put these sentences in the right order.
 (a) She began to tell lies and to be rude.
 (b) She knew 400 signs and could talk about a lot of things.
 (c) Now she is using words.
 (d) Koko learned to ask for food and drink.
 (e) She can talk about pictures in books, and she is beginning to read words.
 (f) She began to think of her own new signs.
 (g) With the help of her special machines she can make the sounds of human speech.
 (h) She learned to use signs for ideas too.

Make a paragraph from the sentences.
Begin your sentences with these words:
1 First   2 Soon   3 Then   4 Next   8 So

C Read for detail
1 How old is Koko?
2 Does she live in an African zoo?
3 What's the name of Penny's friend?
4 What's the name of Penny's other gorilla?
5 Find examples in the text of:
 (a) a lie   (b) a new sign   (c) two rude words

D What do you think?
1 Can Koko talk?
2 Does Penny Patterson have an easy job?

E Read for language
1 Put these words into two groups:
 words for things   words for ideas
 food   drink   more   hungry   fruit   ball
 him   bad   finger   sad   happy   mouth   you
 cigarette   today   tomorrow   teeth   eye

2 Find the past tense forms of these verbs:
 teach   can   take   run   bite   is   put   make
 come   see   mean   say   know   find   think

3 Match a sentence in A with another in B. Then join the two sentences with 'so'.
 Example: Koko was angry with Penny *so* she was very rude to her.
 A Deaf people often can't speak well
   Gorillas can't make human sounds
   A visitor took Koko's ball
   Koko was angry with Penny
   Koko tells lies
 B She bit him
   She was very rude to her
   They talk with their hands
   She is really using language
   Penny taught Koko sign language

F Do you know?
 Gorillas in the wild do not fight.
 They eat only plants.
 They sleep in a different place every night.
 They live for about twenty-five years.

2 ROOM FOR ONE

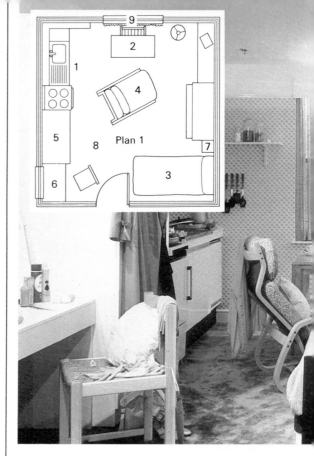

Young people often leave their family home and go to work in another town. Then they have to find the first home of their own – one room. Near the end of their lives old people too leave the family home. Their children have left, and their wives or husbands have died. They don't need a large house, and they don't like an empty house. So they move into the home of one of their children – to a 'granny flat' or a room of their own. So, both the first home and the last home are often just one room, or a 'bed-sitter'. But, for both young and old, one room can be a real home. You can have a good life in a bed-sitter, but you must design it well for one-person living. These two rooms for one are full of good ideas.

A home in a room . . . for Granny

Old people want to be near their families but they don't want to be with them all the time. The answer is a room of their own, on the ground floor. In this bed-sitting room Granny can be completely private, or she can open her door and talk to other people. She can cook her own breakfast and supper, or she can eat with her family. Her grandchildren come and talk to her after school, or she goes upstairs and reads their bed-time story. Mother and father can go out for the evening and Granny will stay with the children. It's a good life for all the family.

This room was once the family dining room. Now, with a special little kitchen area and new furniture, it's a complete home for Granny. The room is in two parts, for daytime and night-time. The daytime end, near the window, has a little kitchen with a small refrigerator and a cooker. There is a table under the window for meals. She can write

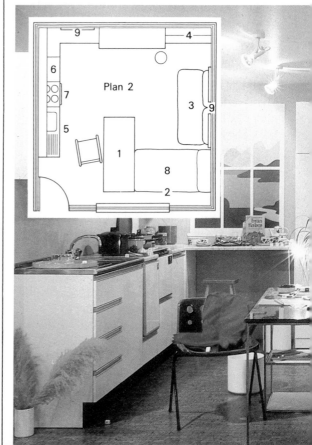

for granny

for a student

letters there and do other things too. The armchair is very modern but very comfortable. Granny can sit in front of the fire and watch her favourite programmes on her own small television. A large wardrobe on the left-hand wall holds all her clothes and divides the living from the sleeping area. There are big drawers under the bed for winter clothes and bed-linen, and a small chest of drawers on the right of the bed for other things. The bed is near the door, so Granny can get to the toilet easily, and she has her own dressing table opposite the bed. The colours are modern but soft and warm – light brown, white and cream. There is a thick carpet from wall to wall, and the green plants make a pretty indoor garden. Granny can clean her room quickly and easily, and it is always nice and tidy. She has brought her favourite pictures, photos and ornaments from her old house, and she always drinks tea from her best china – she has a Wedgwood teaset. She doesn't have her own house but she has a real home. And she has her own family just outside the door.

Life in one room ...
for a student

Students often have to live, sleep, eat, work and play in one single room. This bed-sitter is just right for a student. There is a lot of room for work: a big table and a desk, and shelves for books on the wall. The big cupboards and drawers hide clothes, shoes, papers, and sports things. There are drawers under the bed and the sofa too. A student can work in this room all day, stop for a quick cup of coffee or for lunch, and then have a group of friends to a small party in the evening. Friends can sit on the bed and the sofa, on the green chair or on the floor. They can move the table and dance in the centre of the room.

In the mini-kitchen on the left there is a

13

sink, a small refrigerator, a Baby Belling cooker, and a lot of cupboards and drawers for plates, cups and saucers, knives, forks, spoons, glasses and cooking things. There are strong lights over the kitchen wall and the sitting area, and two good lamps in the corner. The bed is very comfortable and the dark brown duvet is always smart. A student can quickly make the bed in the morning and tidy the sitting area. Then the room is ready for work or for visitors. The two windows are not real ones. They are pictures of windows and bring the idea of the country into this one-room city home. You can easily copy this idea, or you can cover the walls with pictures and photos from magazines. Any student can make a nice home from this kind of room, and will never want to leave. This first home is first-class.

Studio Solo – the new home for one

Now there's a new idea for solo living – your own studio. The idea for Studio Solo came from Sir Lawrie Barratt. 'I built my own house with my own hands in 1953,' says Sir Lawrie, 'and now I'm building houses for other people – 14,000 a year. I have never forgotten the need of young people for a home of their own. 70% of Barratt houses are for first-time buyers. Young people want small, cheap homes, so we build one or two-bedroom flats and houses. We are always asking, "What kind of people need new houses? What kind of homes do they want?"'

Barratt have found a large group of people without real homes, the 4,000,000 single people in Britain. They wanted real homes, not just bed-sitters, so Barratt designed Studio Solo. Studio Solo is the new single-person home for house-buyers of all ages. It is a complete home for one. It has a large living area, 4.460 m × 2.880 m, a real kitchen, 2.600 m × 1.825 m, a private shower and toilet, and a dressing area. You open your own front door into the living area. There is a small table near the door, and on the left-hand wall there is a comfortable sofa-bed in brown. In the daytime it's a sofa and at night it's a bed. Opposite the door there is a dining table with two chairs. There are shelves for your books, cupboards for your china and glass, and a

Sir Lawrie Barratt builds 14,000 homes a year.

special unit for your TV or Hi-Fi. A light brown carpet covers the floor of the living area and there are white tiles on the kitchen floor and walls. The furniture is modern and very smart. You will find good cupboards, a cooker and a refrigerator in the kitchen. And you can wash all your clothes at home – there's a small washing machine next to the sink and a tumble dryer under the linen cupboard. In the dressing area there is a large wardrobe, a chest of drawers and a dressing table. You can shut the door to the dressing area, so the living area is always tidy. There's a comfortable armchair too, and curtains at the windows. You just bring in your cups and saucers, pictures and

14

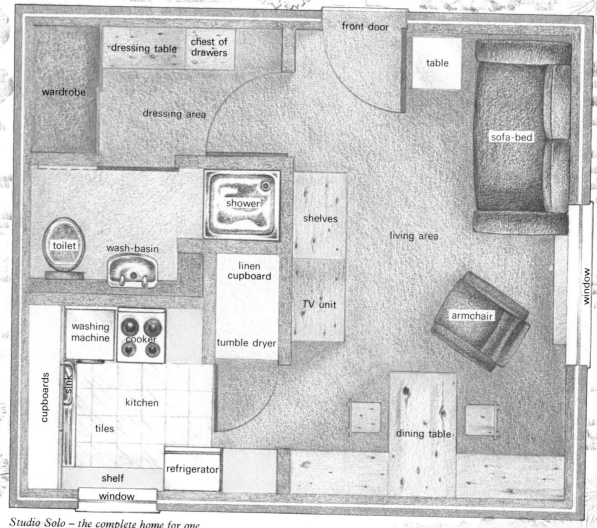

Studio Solo – the complete home for one.

ornaments, and your home is ready.

Do you need a lot of money to buy a Studio Solo? Barratt say, 'We build real homes for people, and they are cheap. And you can easily borrow the money to buy a Studio Solo. After twenty-five years it will be yours. A bed-sitter won't be.' You don't have to buy any furniture for a Studio Solo. You won't need money for a cooker or a refrigerator, for a carpet or curtains. It's all there, in the complete home for one. Barratt build Studio Solos in groups of four on one floor or next to one-bedroom flats. They are in the centre of cities, near the shops, cinemas and schools. Single people with good jobs can have a good life in these new homes for one.

The smallest room in the world?

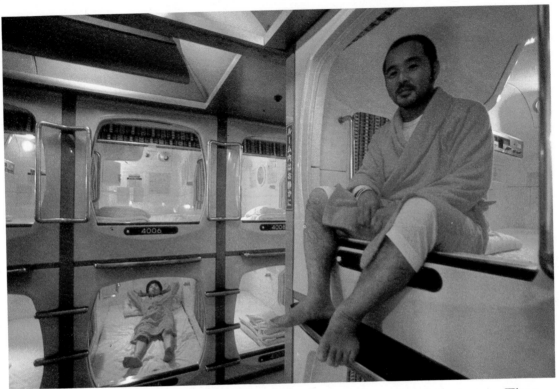

Do you just want a room for one night? Then the Japanese have found the answer. They have designed the smallest room in the world for their 'capsule hotels'. You go straight through a small door into your bed. You have your own little washbasin, radio, telephone, clock and TV – and a toothbrush. A capsule is very cheap, but it is not a room for life. It's only a room for one night.

Exercises

A Before you read
1 Look at the photos of rooms on p. 12 and 13, and the studio on p. 15. What do you think of the design of these homes for one?

2 Would you like to live in one of these homes? Why/Why not?

B Read for ideas
1 Complete this summary. The first letter of each word will help you.

'Both y... and old people can have a g... life in a bed-sitter. O... people like a r... in one of their children's homes, but students often move to a new t.... The two bed-sitters show many good i... for solo living. The f... is modern and comfortable, and there is a small k... area. People can soon make a real h... in these rooms for one. But some single p... do not want to l... in a bed-sitter. They w... a larger home with a r... kitchen and their own shower and toilet. They can now b... a Studio Solo, the new k... of home for s... people of all a....'

2 Compare the two bed-sitters. Put S for student, G for granny or B for both after these sentences.
   (a) There are a lot of cupboards and drawers.
   (b) There is a small TV.
   (c) There is an indoor garden.
   (d) There is a small cooker and refrigerator.
   (e) There are good, strong lights for work.
   (f) There is a desk and bookshelves.
   (g) Your own family is outside the door.
   (h) You can easily tidy the room.
   (i) You can dance in the centre of the room.

C Read for detail
1 What does Granny read to her grandchildren?
2 What does she put in the drawers under the bed?
3 Where does the student put sports things?
4 How many single people are there in Britain?
5 Work out the area of the studio kitchen.
6 Do you need to buy curtains for a Studio?

D Talk about homes
Put these ideas in order: 1 for best → 5 for worst. Compare your order with other students and give your reasons.
The right place for an old person is:
(a) in their own house
(b) in a special home for old people
(c) in a hospital
(d) in a room in one of their children's homes
(e) in a one-bedroom flat

E Read for language
1 You have just moved into a one-bedroom flat. There is one wrong piece of furniture in each room. Which is it? Where does it really belong? Make new lists.

Kitchen	Bathroom	Living room	Bedroom
table	cupboard	refrigerator	drawers
wardrobe	chair	armchair	dressing-
washing-	bed	desk	table
machine		sofa	cooker

2 Join these phrases:
   You cook food   in a washing machine
   You keep food   in a cooker
   You dry clothes   in a refrigerator
   You wash clothes   in a tumble dryer

3 Describe the kitchen on p. 15. Study the plan. Begin: *On the right of the door there is ....* Use these prepositions: *in front of   behind on the right/left of   next to   near   under*

F Describe and draw
Work in pairs, Student A and Student B.
Both draw a plan of a room in your home, but do not show your partner.
Student A: Describe your room to your partner.
Student B: Draw a plan of Student A's room.
Change over.
Student A draw B's room. Compare your plans.

3 IT'S PANTOMIME TIME

A family at the pantomime, Christmas 1871.

(above) Characters from the Commedia dell' Arte – from left to right, Pantaloon, Harlequin, Columbine, Clown. (right) Joseph Grimaldi (1778–1837) – the first Joey the Clown.

It's a cold, winter night but, in the theatre, people are warm and happy. The children sit with their parents and wait for the fun to begin. At last the lights go out and the curtain goes up. Suddenly Joey the Clown jumps onto the stage.

'Here we are again,' he cries. 'Hello, children.'

'Hello,' a small girl answers.

'I can't hear you,' says Joey. 'Louder please. Hello, children.'

'Hello,' all the boys and girls answer.

'Again,' says Joey. 'Really loudly this time. Hello, children.'

'Hello,' all the children shout.

'How are you tomorrow?' asks Joey.

All the people in the audience laugh. 'It's *today*,' they shout.

Then a fat old woman comes onto the stage. 'Good evening, children,' she says in a man's voice. 'Have you been good today?'

'Yes, we have,' the children shout.

Who is Joey? Who is this woman with a man's voice? What's happening in the theatre? It's pantomime time. In the weeks after Christmas British theatres are full of families. They have all come to see the pantomime. Pantomime is part of a real British Christmas.

What is a pantomime?

A pantomime tells a story, an old story, a children's story – *Cinderella, Dick Whittington and his Cat*, or *Aladdin and his Lamp*. A pantomime is full of music and dance, but it is not an opera or a ballet. There are often clowns or animals in a pantomime, but it is not a circus. A pantomime is . . . a pantomime. A good pantomime is very funny, but there is often a lesson in it too. Good people have to fight bad people, but they always win in the end. So children learn about Right and Wrong and True Love. And they have a good time in the theatre. They can laugh, shout and sing. It's all part of a real pantomime.

'pantomimus' never spoke but used his body, face and hands to tell a story. This use of mime has always been part of pantomime.

Pantomime has roots in Italian theatre too, in the *Commedia dell'Arte* of the sixteenth and seventeenth centuries. Groups of actors travelled round Italy and France and told stories through words and mime. The characters were always the same – Harlequin, a poor but clever young man, Columbine, a pretty girl, and Pantaloon, her father. He is a nasty old man and has a servant, Clown. Harlequin loves Columbine and wants to marry her. Pantaloon says, 'No,' so Harlequin and Columbine run away together. Pantaloon and Clown try to catch them, but Clown is really helping Harlequin. Together they play a lot of tricks on the stupid old man, and he never catches the young lovers. Harlequin has a magic stick, so he can quickly change people and things. Tricks and quick changes are an important part of a modern pantomime.

When was the first English pantomime?

The *Commedia dell'Arte* came to England at the end of the seventeenth century and London actors copied its ideas. One famous actor, John Rich, had his own theatre in London, and in 1721 he produced a play about Harlequin. His funny story about Harlequin and Columbine had music and magic tricks. It was the first English pantomime.

Pantomime is always changing. In the nineteenth century there was a famous clown, Joseph Grimaldi. He played a lot of clever tricks, he sang songs with the audience, and he told good jokes. People came to see Joey the Clown in the pantomime. He was the real hero, not Harlequin.

Where does pantomime come from?

Pantomime has its roots in the ancient world of Greece and Rome. In Rome there was a big winter festival, the *Saturnalia*. The ancient Romans ate and drank a lot, and danced in the streets. Women wore men's clothes and men wore women's clothes. Slaves gave orders to their masters, and masters served their slaves. In a modern pantomime women play men's parts and men dress in women's clothes. The servants have a lot of power.

The word 'pantomime' comes from Greece and Rome too. 'Pantomimus' was the Latin name for a special kind of actor. The

(above) Aladdin and the Princess with the Genie of the Magic Lamp.
(left) An ugly man must always be the Pantomime Dame.

What's in a modern pantomime?

A modern pantomime is full of these ideas from the past: music, mime, dance, tricks and jokes. The audience laugh and sing, and shout at the actors on the stage. People know the story and wait for their favourite characters to appear. *Aladdin* is a good example of a pantomime. The story comes from *The Arabian Nights* and is hundreds of years old. First there is the hero, or Principal Boy, Aladdin. The Principal Boy must be a young woman, or perhaps a Pop Star. Then there is Aladdin's mother, Widow Twankey. Her husband is dead, so she has to wash clothes for money. Widow Twankey is the Pantomime Dame, and an ugly man must play this funny part. She has another son, Wishee Washee, and a horse. This horse can talk and dance. It isn't a real horse, but two men. One actor is the front legs, the other the back. There is a beautiful princess, too, the Principal Girl, and she has two slave-girls. Pretty young women play all these parts.

One day Aladdin meets a strange old man, Abanazar. Abanazar says to Aladdin, 'I am your father's brother.' But he is really a wicked magician, the Villain of the pantomime. He gives Aladdin a ring and takes him to an old, dry well. 'Go down the well and through the door at the bottom,' he tells Aladdin. 'You will find a lamp in a cave under the ground. Bring it back to me.' Aladdin finds the lamp but doesn't give it to Abanazar. He jumps out of the well and runs home. Widow Twankey tries to rub the dirt off the lamp and – magic – the Genie of the Lamp appears. The Genie helps Aladdin and his family. Aladdin is going to marry the Princess and live in a palace. Then, one day, Abanazar comes back . . .

A scene from Aladdin

So Shi and Sing Hi, the princess's slave girls enter with an Arabian chest.

Princess:	Thank you, So Shi and you, Sing Hi. Is this my luggage for the honeymoon?
Slave girls:	Yes, Your Highness.
Princess:	Have I got all my clothes? I must look. *So Shi opens the chest and the Princess goes through the clothes.* Morning dress, afternoon dress, evening dress, sixty-eight pairs of shoes. . . Oh! Who put this old lamp in here? *The slave girls do not know, so the Princess holds up the lamp.* Auuuuuuurrcch – it's very dirty. It'll mark all my lovely new dresses.
Abanazar:	(*off*) New lamps for old! New lamps for old!
So Shi:	Listen! It's an old pedlar. He's selling lamps. *Abanazar enters. He is wearing pedlar's clothes and carrying a lot of lamps.*
Abanazar:	New lamps for old! New lamps for old!
Princess:	New lamps for old. That's a strange kind of business.
Abanazar:	I have my reasons, my dear.
Princess:	(*laughs*) Well, they're very strange reasons, *I* think.
Abanazar:	They are, my dear. They are. New lamps for old! (*to the audience, angrily*) Tell her to hurry up.
Princess:	Well, we need a lamp, but I want a *clean* one on my honeymoon.
Abanazar:	(*holds one out*) Then here you are, my dear.
Princess:	That's lovely! Why does Aladdin want this dirty old thing? (*to the slave girls*) Shall I give it to the nice old pedlar?
Slave girls:	Yes, Your Highness.
Princess:	(*asks the audience*) Shall I?
Audience:	NO!
Abanazar:	(*from behind his hand, to the audience, very angrily*) Yes, you stupid fools. Yes!
Audience:	NO!
Princess:	No? Oh, it'll be all right. A new lamp will be a big surprise for my husband.
Abanazar:	It'll be a big surprise, because – (*He seizes the lamp from her*) I am Abanazar. *Screams from the slave girls.*
Princess:	(*screams*) Aaaaaaaaah *Abanazar rubs the lamp. The Genie enters.* *Abanazar speaks very loudly.*
Abanazar:	Make Aladdin's palace fly through the air. And take us to Egypt, take us there. *Abanazar pulls the Princess off the stage and the palace disappears.*

In the end Aladdin gets back his lamp, his palace and his princess. And Abanazar? He has to wash clothes for Widow Twankey.

The washing song from *Aladdin*.

Wishee Washee, will you wash my washing nice and bright?
Wishee Washee, will you wash my wash, and wash it white?
Wishee Washee, will you wash my washing right away?
Or Wishee Washee, will you wish to wash my wash another day?

It's the end of the show,
Time for us all to go,
Hope we'll see you all next time,
'Cos★ it's the end of this year's pantomime,
Goodbye and cheers,
Many happy new years,
And that's the end of the show!

★ 'Cos = Because

Notes

slave servants and slaves both work for another person but slaves do not get any money.

pedlar a pedlar goes from place to place and sells small things.

honeymoon a special holiday for a new husband and wife.

Exercises

A Before you read

1 What do you always find in a ballet, a play, an opera, a circus – singers, dancers, clowns, actors?
2 Look at the pictures on p. 18–20. Have you seen people like them before? If so, when and where?

B Read for ideas

Mark the sentences below True or False.
Then correct the false sentences and copy the true ones to make a paragraph.

1 People go to the pantomime in summer.
2 Pantomimes are for all the family.
3 They tell an old children's story.
4 A pantomime is never funny so the audience has a bad time in the theatre.
5 They can laugh, shout and sing.
6 The wrong people always win in the end.

C Read for detail

1 Copy and complete these notes with the words below

C4 B.C.	Ancient . . . . . 'Pantomimus' – mime. Saturnalia – dance. men ↔ women masters ↔ servants
C16 and C17	. . . . . and France *Commedia dell'Arte* Story of . . . ., magic stick, quick changes and . . . . .
End C17 1721	England. London. John Rich. 1st English . . . . . music, ... tricks.
C19	Joey the . . . . . → hero. tricks, jokes and . . . . .
C20	Pop . . . . . = Principal Boy

clown   Harlequin   Italy   magic   mime
tricks   pantomime   songs   star   world

2 What is strange about a pantomime horse?
3 What was special about Aladdin's lamp?
4 Find two examples of tricks in the story of Aladdin.

D What do you think?

1 Why did Abanazar give Aladdin a ring?
2 Why didn't Abanazar go down the well?
3 Why didn't Aladdin give Abanazar the lamp?

E Read for language

1 Find the opposites of these words:

ugly   daughter   right   good   father   dirty
wife   stupid   nice   villain   Prince   boy

Make two lists of pairs like this:

+	−		♂	♀
good	bad		boy	girl

2 Retell the story of Aladdin. Use the past tense of all verbs *not* between '. . .' Begin: Once upon a time there *was* an old woman called Widow Twankey. She *had* two sons . . . End: One day Abanazar *came* back.

F Practical Reading

Study this newspaper advertisement.

SHAFTESBURY, Shaftesbury Ave.
THE THEATRE OF COMEDY
COMPANY PRESENTS
Spectacular Family Christmas Pantomime
ALADDIN
WITH ALL-STAR CAST.
OPENS DECEMBER 16.
Reduced prices for all performances if
booked and paid for before August 31.
£7·50, £6·00, £4·50. Box office 01-
836 6596 or 01-836 4255. Credit card
hotline 01-930 9232.
Group sales 379 6061.

1 Which theatre is *Aladdin* at?
2 Which street is the theatre in?
3 What is Xmas short for?
4 When is the first performance?
5 What is the telephone number of the box office?
6 Can you pay by credit card?
7 What is the last date for cheap tickets?
8 What will it cost to book tickets for a family of five at the lowest price?

4 ALL LIFE IS THERE ...

One day a professor of archaeology walked into his class and put an empty beer can on the table. Then he said to his students, 'You are archaeologists in the year 3982. You have just found this strange object from the past. Look at it, and think about it. Talk to your friends about it. What kind of people used this object? What kind of society did it come from? Right. You have half an hour.' He left the room.

For the first time the students really understood the work of archaeologists. They often have to build a picture of a past society from one small object.

Archaeologists at work.

...IN A TIME CAPSULE

Archaeologists will have an easier time in the future. People of the twentieth century are burying **time capsules** – special boxes full of objects from today's world. Dr Thornton Jacobs buried the first time capsule at Atlanta, Georgia, in 1935. He put small models of people, houses and furniture inside it, with examples of food and drink, and a record of President Roosevelt's voice. At the New York World Fair in 1939 there was a time capsule with a message inside it from Albert Einstein. And for the great Expo at Osaka in 1970 the Japanese made a capsule full of information about the whole world. With modern micro-technology they were able to include the grammar of seven hundred languages!

Now there is a British time capsule. On Wednesday, November 17th 1982, the BBC buried their special time capsule in the gardens of Castle Howard in Yorkshire. The steel capsule is small, but very strong. It is now deep underground in a special concrete 'room' with steel walls. The capsule must stay there for two thousand years. Then, in 3982, people will be able to open it again and look at all the things inside.

Castle Howard, Yorkshire. The BBC Time Capsule lies deep underground in the gardens.

What did the BBC put in the capsule? 'We wanted to give a picture of today's world to people of the future,' they say. 'So we put in all kinds of things from twentieth-century life. First we got all the newspapers for one day, July 21st, and their circulation figures. Then we chose examples of magazines: weekly and monthly ones, women's magazines and children's comics, magazines on sport or politics, on money or hobbies. We put all these newspapers and magazines on microfilm – and we've put a large magnifying glass in the capsule, too. They won't have the same machines in 3982, but people will be able to read the microfilm with the magnifying glass.

'Next we thought about television. People today watch a lot of television, so we put in six hours of typical BBC programmes: *Man Alive*, *Playschool*, *20th Century Remembered*, *Nationwide*, and the *News*. We also found room for some pages of Ceefax and some of the advertisements from ITV. All these examples of TV are on videodisc. Radio programmes are important too, so we made slow speed audio discs of programmes from Radio 3 and Radio 4. Radio 3 is the classical music programme, and we asked Professor Michael Tilmouth of Edinburgh to make a list of works for the capsule.'

Professor Tilmouth: 'I listened to all the music programmes on Radio 3 on October 6th 1982. I wanted to include important examples of classical music, but there were only two really great works that day – Beethoven's *Symphony No 7*, and Brahms' *Piano Concerto No 2*. From Haydn we had a flute trio – not one of his great piano trios. I also chose the slow movement of Mozart's *Symphony No 29 in A* and the first movement of his *Piano Concerto No 23 in A*. I wanted to show great performers too, so there are records of Arthur Rubinstein and Janet Baker. Rubinstein is

A magnifying glass.

4.10
Who is Sappho?
Over 2,500 years ago on the Greek island of Lesbos, Sappho lived and flourished as a lyric poet, and ever since her work has been acclaimed by writers and scholars. Frank Delaney, in conversation with the poet **Judith Kazantzis** and two classical scholars, **Professor Mary Lefkowitz** and **Dr Angus Bowie**, seeks out the woman beyond the myths and her poems which still speak directly to us today.
Lyre music
DR CHRISTOPHER PAGE
Reader BARBARA JEFFORD
Producer SUSAN DENNY
(Repeat)

7.0 News

7.5 The Archers
(*Repeated: Wed 1.40 pm*)

7.20 Medicine Now
Geoff Watts reports on the health of medical care – from the research laboratory and the operating theatre to the dentist's chair and the GP's surgery.
Producer ALISON RICHARDS
(Repeated: Sat 2.35 pm)

7.50 File on 4
Major issues, changing attitudes, important events at home and abroad.
Reporter Roger Finnigan
Producer PAUL CAMPBELL
Editor DAVID TAYLOR
BBC Manchester

The 'Radio Times' – for TV and radio programmes.

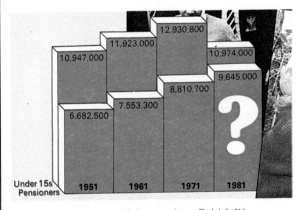
Statistics – for facts and figures about British life.

playing piano music by Schumann and Janet Baker is singing some of Schubert's songs. Oh, I put in a tuning fork too, so people will be able to hear our idea of A.'

What about popular music? 'We didn't

A tuning fork.

A page of Ceefax – for news and information.

A typical 1980s photo – a pop concert.

From Radio 4 there are examples of talks: *Science Now*, *Medicine Now*, a programme about a sixteenth-century ship, the *Mary Rose*, and a talk about women writers past and present. In this talk, Susan Denny spoke about Sappho, a Greek woman poet from 600 B.C.

'Sappho is a good choice for the capsule,' she says. 'She was one of a group of women writers in Ancient Greece, but her work disappeared for centuries. Then, two thousand years after her death, someone discovered copies of her poems in the dry sands of North Africa. Today we have a group of good women writers, and two thousand years from now people will discover their work again – in the capsule. Some lines from a favourite Sappho poem have just the right message for the capsule:

> Make no mistake, the Golden Muse
>   brought good fortune,
> And after my death, people will
>   remember me.
> Let me tell you this –
> Someone in some future time will think
>   of me.'

For drama, the BBC chose a modern play by Frederick Raphael about the ancient Greek story of Daedalus. This play is on one of the cassettes in the capsule. Other cassettes give examples of programmes from local radio. So there is a full picture of the media in the 1980s – newspapers, TV, radio and disc.

There is also a long list of books, all on microfilm, and a lot of information about life today. There are copies of the *Annual Abstract of Statistics* – facts and figures about British life from 1840 to 1980 – and the results of a Gallup Poll on people's values. Health was at the top of the list, then the family, but sex and politics were both near the bottom.

Jenny Calder of the Royal Scottish

forget popular music. We put in all the records from *Top 40* on Radio 1 on October 10th. So people of the future will be able to hear favourite pop songs of the twentieth century.'

27

1 pottery   **4** jewel   **7** tools   **10** golf ball
2 beer can   **5** map   **8** toy cars
3 packets of seeds   **6** plan   **9** money

Museum chose the photos to go with the statistics. 'I looked for photos of buildings, of homes and family life, love and marriage, holidays and work, school life, free time, clothes, shops and transport. I also wanted to show some general ideas – the place of women in society, the differences between town and country life, national traditions, and *our* idea of the twentieth century. One photo can often show different things. For example, in a photo of family life, people are usually wearing clothes. And there are often people in photos of buildings. So, all the photos give a lot of information.'

An archaeologist, Peter Warren, chose objects for the capsule. 'Things had to be small, strong, typical and beautiful,' he says. 'Archaeologists love beautiful "finds" from the past. And they want to know all about the people and their society. How did they live? What did they do? What did they value? So I chose objects for future archaeologists. I included some packets of seeds. They will tell archaeologists about our food, our gardens and farms. I put in money and tools, pottery – that always lasts for centuries – a beautiful jewel and a golf ball. All these objects are typical of our life today.

'I have tried to make the work of future archaeologists easier. They will find maps of the world, plans of our cities and photos from the air. We also included a map of the stars in November 1982. This will give the date of the capsule. Twentieth-century archaeologists have learnt a lot about life in Ancient Egypt and China from the toys and models in their tombs. So I have included toy cars, model aeroplanes, that kind of thing. They will tell fortieth-century archaeologists about children's toys *and* the adult world. And I didn't forget to put in a beer can!'

Notes

BBC British Broadcasting Corporation. The BBC has national and local television and radio stations.
ITV Independent Television. Its money comes from advertisements.

muse the muses of ancient Greece gave poets their ideas.
Gallup poll a special count of people's answers to questions about society.

Exercises

A Before you read
1 What do you know about daily life in your country two thousand years ago? How do you know about it?
2 What will a beer can tell people of the future about society today?

B Read for ideas
Choose the best answer:
1 Archaeologists
  (a) look after objects from the past
  (b) teach students about the past
  (c) study societies of the past

2 The first time capsule was
  (a) an American idea
  (b) a Japanese idea
  (c) a British idea

3 Objects for a time capsule must be
  (a) typical of daily life
  (b) cheap but beautiful
  (c) examples of microtechnology

4 There are examples of TV programmes in the British time capsule because
  (a) the BBC makes TV programmes
  (b) television is an important part of modern life
  (c) TV programmes give a full picture of twentieth-century society.

5 Archaeologists of the future will know the date of the capsule from
  (a) photos and plans
  (b) lists of books and statistics
  (c) a map of the stars

C Read for detail
1 Study the photos on p. 26 and 27.
  (a) What is the magnifying glass for?
  (b) Why is there a tuning fork?
  (c) What changes in the British population do the statistics show?
  (d) What will the photo of a pop festival tell people about clothes, music, etc.?
  (e) At what time can you hear the News?

2 Find the names of these people:
  (a) He wrote a play about Daedalus.
  (b) She works in a museum.
  (c) He is a professor of music.
  (d) He was President of the USA.
  (e) She wrote poems long ago.
  (f) He wrote flute and piano trios.
  (g) He is an archaeologist.

3 Match the kind of programmes to the right radio station: *Radio 1, Radio 3, Radio 4* – Talks, popular music, classical music.

D What do you think?
1 Why is the work of archaeologists difficult?
2 Do the objects in the BBC capsule give a good picture of 20th-century life?
3 Make your own lists of objects for a time capsule. Give reasons for your choice.

E Read for language
1 Put these words into three groups:
  (a) print   (b) audio   (c) visual
cassettes lists photos magazines audio-discs maps books records newspapers videodiscs statistics

2 You find the same words in different languages. *Example:* **radio**. Which words in this text are the same in your language? Make a list.

3 Identify these objects on p. 28:
  (a) It's very small and beautiful. You must pay a lot of money for it.
  (b) It's metal with round ends and straight sides. You pull a ring to open it.

4 Choose three objects from the capsule. Describe the shape, colour, size, etc.
Ask another student to identify them.

F Class poll
What do people value? Put this list in order 1–10. What are the class results?
Politics, friends, work, health, money, sport, sex, hobbies, family life, holidays.

5 BIRDMEN
ANCIENT AND MODERN

From the beginning of time to the present day people have wanted to fly. They could swim like fish in the sea, but they could not fly through the air like birds. Many people made wings and tried to fly. Some never got off the ground and up into the air. Others jumped from the tops of hills or houses, and quickly fell to their death. But men have always hoped to become birds or birdmen. The first and most famous story of birdmen comes from Ancient Greece.

The story of Icarus

Once upon a time, in Ancient Greece, there lived a wonderful craftsman, Daedalus. The people of Athens looked at his statues and said, 'Daedalus makes statues like real people. They almost breathe and move. He is the cleverest craftsman in the whole world.' Daedalus taught many young pupils, and one of them, Talus, had many good ideas. People began to say, 'Talus is cleverer than his master.' Daedalus grew very jealous.

One dark night Daedalus killed Talus and fled from the city of Athens. He escaped to the island of Crete and worked for the king, Minos. Minos told Daedalus to make a special prison for the minotaur, a dangerous monster, half-man and half-bull. So Daedalus built the famous labyrinth of Minos, and the Cretans kept their fierce monster inside it.

Minos, king of Crete, did not want to lose his clever craftsman, so he threw Daedalus into his own prison, the labyrinth. And he put Daedalus' young son, Icarus, in prison with his father. Daedalus had to find a way to escape. He knew all the paths of the labyrinth, but the fierce minotaur guarded the way out. Daedalus sat and thought. Icarus played by his side. 'Look,' cried Icarus suddenly. 'Look at that pretty bird!' Daedalus raised his head,

but the bird was afraid. It flew up into the sky and out of the labyrinth.

Daedalus had an idea. 'Birds can fly in and out of the labyrinth,' he thought. 'If I make wings for myself and Icarus, we too can fly out of this prison.' So Daedalus got feathers and wax, and made wings for himself and his son. Then, in the middle of the night, father and son flew silently up and out of the labyrinth. Like birds they flew, up, up into the sky. Like birds they flew through the dark night, away from the angry king in his dangerous island.

The sky began to grow light. 'Be careful,' called Daedalus to Icarus. 'Apollo, the sun, is waking up. Do not go near him. His breath is hot and it will melt your wings.' But Icarus did not hear his father. He saw the beautiful sun in the east and flew towards it. The heat melted the wax in his wings, and the feathers began to fall, one by one, to the water below. Icarus was afraid. He beat his thin wings faster. He tried to fly away from the sun's hot breath, but it was too late. The last of the feathers dropped from his back. Like a stone he fell, down, down into the sea. The people of the world have never forgotten Icarus. His name lives on in the Icarian Sea, and men still try to fly like birds.

Icarus flies too near the sun. The heat melts the wax and the feathers fall from his wings.

In the twentieth century the skies are full of metal birds – aeroplanes – full of people. But passengers in planes are not flying like birds. They just sit in a large metal box and flying power comes from jet engines. People still try to become real birdmen. Some turn to the new sport of hang-gliding. Others are designing new kinds of wings which will help men to fly. And now the dreams are beginning to come true.

23rd August 1977

£50,000 reward to birdman

Today Dr Paul MacCready of California is a happy man. He has just won a £50,000 reward for his man-powered plane, *Gossamer Condor*. With a team of scientists and craftsmen he has worked for months on his special plane. It has wings, but there is no motor of any kind. All its power comes from one man. The pilot pedals the plane like a bicycle. Last week the plane made its first flight. It flew up into the sky and stayed up for a whole hour.

The £50,000 comes from British businessman, Henry Kremer. 'This is wonderful news,' he said last night. 'All my dreams are coming true.' And he immediately offered a new reward. 'I'll give £100,000 to the first person to cross the Channel in a man-powered plane,' he promised. So it's back to work tomorrow for Dr MacCready and his team.

7th June 1979

American team try for Cross-Channel prize

Two years ago a team of scientists in America won a £50,000 reward from Henry Kremer for making the first man-powered flight. Now they are ready for the next prize of £100,000. They have built a new plane, the *Gossamer Albatross*, and brought it to Britain. The *Gossamer Albatross* looks like a large bird or a strange kind of plane. It is really a flying bicycle.

The team leader, Dr MacCready has made all the arrangements. He has chosen a flight path with the help of both British and French officials. He has solved last-minute problems. On a test flight in May one wing broke, but his team soon designed and made a new one. In two weeks the plane was ready for the real test flight – across the Channel. On 4th June they took the plane to Folkestone, and now it's ready and waiting – for the right weather.

Birdman Bryan Allen

The pilot, Bryan Allen, talked to our reporter.

Smith: You're a student, aren't you?

Allen: Yes, that's right. But I'm also a cyclist, and I've done some hang-gliding.

Smith: Haven't you won some cycling races in the USA?

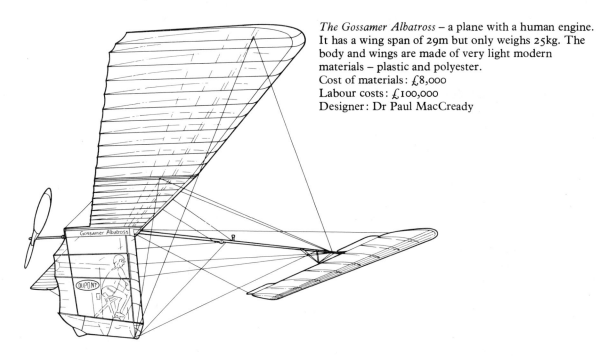

The Gossamer Albatross – a plane with a human engine. It has a wing span of 29m but only weighs 25kg. The body and wings are made of very light modern materials – plastic and polyester.
Cost of materials: £8,000
Labour costs: £100,000
Designer: Dr Paul MacCready

Bryan Allen at the pedals of his special plane.

Allen: Several, but I only race in my free time. It keeps me fit.

Smith: Do you need to be very fit to fly the *Albatross*?

Allen: Sure. I have an exercise programme and I work through it every day. If I get tired on the flight, I'll crash. So I do my exercises.

Smith: But why are you doing this flight? Is it for science or just for fun?

Allen: Well, science *is* fun, when you work with this kind of team.

Smith: Are you afraid?

Allen: No, not really. There'll be hundreds of boats which can pick me up, and I *can* swim! The real problem is the weather. I need low winds, about ten kph, a low temperature and very good visibility. I'll have to fly low, only about nine metres above the water, so I must be able to see. That's unusual weather for the Channel, those things together.

Smith: Well, I hope you get a good day soon. And the best of luck.

Allen: Thanks.

Across the Channel in a flying bicycle

Bryan Allen, 26, flew across the Channel today in 2 hours 49 minutes. A slow time? Not when you are flying a bicycle with wings. Bryan took off from Folkestone at 5.50 a.m. and landed on a beach near Cap Griz Nez at 8.39 a.m. His first words? 'I'm thirsty.'

Bryan will get part of the £100,000 prize for the first person to fly across the channel on manpower only. The rest of the money goes to the team of American scientists and craftsmen who built the *Gossamer Albatross*. But Bryan gets all the fame. He is the first birdman in the world.

Exercises

A Before you read

1 Do you know the dates of the first
   (a) aeroplane flight
   (b) cross-channel flight
   (c) man-powered flight
   (d) man-powered cross-channel flight?

2 Quickly look through p. 32–34. Which dates can you find? (*Answers: see p. 96*)

B Read for reasons

Explain the following statements with information from the text. Begin each reason with *Because* . . .
1 Daedalus fled to Crete from Athens.
2 Minos told Daedalus to make a labyrinth.
3 Minos put Daedalus and Icarus in prison.
4 They could not escape on foot.
5 Daedalus decided to make wings for himself and his son.
6 Icarus flew too near the sun.
7 Icarus fell into the sea.

C What do you think?

   (a) Why did Henry Kremer offer £150,000 prize money for man-powered flights?
   (b) Is Dr MacCready now a rich man?
   (c) Why did the flight take place so early?
   (d) Why was Allen thirsty after his flight?

D Check the facts

1 Find a map of the channel and mark the flight path of the *Gossamer Albatross* on it.

2 Fill in the missing dates and then put this diary in the right order.

	Plane to Folkestone
	1st man-powered flight over land
25/5/79	Test flight. One wing broke.
	1st cross-channel man-powered flight.
18/5/79	Fixed flight path.

3 Complete this form for the first Birdman

```
Surname........................
First name.....................
Nationality....................
Age............................
Occupation.....................
Interests.........HANG-GLIDING.
Prizes for.CYCLING.RACES,......
```

E Read for language

1 One word in each group does not belong. Which is it and why?
   (a) angry, jealous, afraid, happy.
   (b) wax, metal, polyester, stone.
   (c) wind, ground, temperature, visibility.
   Choose the right general word for each group: 1) feelings 2) weather 3) materials

2 *Albatross* and *Condor* are both names for
   (a) monsters (b) birds (c) scientists.
   Gossamer means (a) a thick, heavy material
   (b) a thin, light material (c) a strong, modern material.

3 Write a newspaper report about Bryan Allen. Complete this paragraph with the right form of the verb in brackets.
   '. . . **June 11th 1979** Student Bryan Allen is ready for the first man-powered Cross-Channel flight. Allen (win) some cycling races in the USA and (do) some hang-gliding. He (works) through an exercise programme every day to keep fit. If he (get) tired on the flight he (crash). He (do) the flight for fun, and (be) not afraid. He (can) swim and there (be) boats to pick him up. He (need) good visibility, a low temperature and low winds. He (hope) for a good day soon.'
   Can you think of a good headline?

F Find out

What is hang-gliding? Why do people do it? Is it safe?

Is this the most dangerous animal in the world – the Indian tiger? Man-eating tigers used to kill more than 1,000 people a year. Now man has killed nearly all the tigers in the world. Why? Man-eaters today are usually old, sick animals. Most tigers don't hunt people, but hide from them, in deep, dark forests. Or they did. People have cut down the trees, so there aren't many forests for tigers now. People have always hunted, and killed, the tiger. Poor farmers were trying to save their cows and chickens from the night-killer. Rich people just hunted the tiger for fun – and for its beautiful skin. And now poachers are killing the tiger for money – they can easily sell the skin. So, the tiger isn't an enemy of man, but man *is* the enemy of the tiger. All over the world wild animals are in danger from the most dangerous animal of all – man.

The end of the African elephant?

Has the African elephant got a future? Will *your* grandchildren see this wonderful animal? In the last century Africa was full of elephants. In the late 1970s Dr Iain Douglas-Hamilton counted only 1.3 million elephants in the whole of Africa. Thousands of elephants are disappearing every year, and in many game parks there are more dead elephants than live ones. In 1970 there were 20,000 elephants in Uganda. By 1980 there were only about 2,000. This is the sad story of Kabalega Falls National Park in Uganda.

In the 1960s the human population grew very fast and farmers started to take land from the park. They pushed 8,000 elephants into the southern part of Kabalega. Soon the elephant population grew too large for that small area, and began to destroy the bush.

Elephants tear the branches off young trees and eat the leaves. An adult elephant needs one third of a tonne of food a day, and 180 litres of water. If elephants kill too many trees the bush starts to die, and then there is no food or water for any of the wild animals. Parts of Kabalega became deserts, full of dead trees and bones.

The government had to kill some of the elephants to save the park – and the elephants. It was important to get the right balance between land and animals. Then the bush could grow again and feed the elephants and other wild animals. The scheme began well, but then there was a terrible war in Uganda and most people forgot about the game parks. The poachers did not. In the 1970s, when the world price for ivory was very high, poachers killed thousands of Ugandan elephants. After the fall of Idi Amin things grew worse. Ex-soldiers with machine guns became poachers and killed nearly all the elephants. One war in Uganda has ended, but the war against

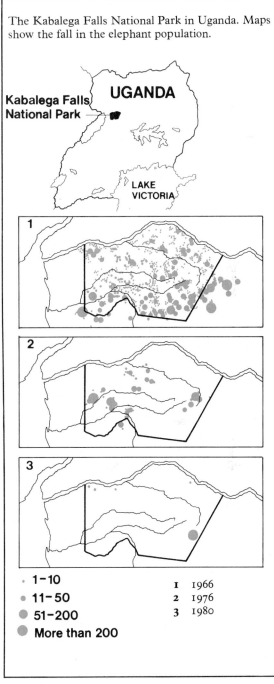

The Kabalega Falls National Park in Uganda. Maps show the fall in the elephant population.

· 1–10
● 11–50
● 51–200
● More than 200

1 1966
2 1976
3 1980

(left) A family of elephants in the African bush. Will poachers kill them for their tusks?

poachers has only just begun. Is there still time to save the elephant? In 1980 there were only 160 elephants in the whole of Kabalega.

When a team of wildlife experts flew over the park they saw a terrible sight. They found a small herd of elephants but the animals went mad with fear and ran wildly from the sound of the plane. To the elephants a plane meant one thing only – death from men with guns. Behind the herd the team could see a line of dead elephants – all without their tusks. The story was the same in Rwenzori Park. On their first day in that park the team heard gunfire. They soon found five dead elephants. No one had taken any meat, or the skins. The poachers had just torn out the tusks. Men used to kill wild animals from fear, for food or for clothes. Now they are killing the elephant for one thing only – money. No one needs ivory but plenty of people want it, and will pay high prices for it. The poachers can always find a market.

In Zimbabwe, government officials are fighting poachers with a new scheme. They are killing elephants themselves, and selling the ivory on the open market. Game warden Mike Drury explains: 'In some parts of Zimbabwe we have too many elephants. There isn't enough land or food for them, and some are getting dangerous. Many elephants died in the terrible drought of 1981/2, but there still isn't enough food for today's herds. We must kill some elephants now or there will be no elephants at all in the future. If we can get the right balance between land, people and animals, then there's hope for the elephant – and for the human population. Money from the sale of skins and ivory goes back to the villages. People get more money if they help the government with the official elephant control scheme. They are learning that poaching doesn't pay.'

New hope for the panda?

In China the government is fighting to save a national treasure – the giant panda. The panda, one of the world's favourite wild animals and one of the rarest, is in great danger. Giant pandas live in the mountains of south-western China. They live in thick forests of fir trees and bamboo, 1,800 to 2,500 metres above sea level. The weather is cold and cloudy, and there is often heavy rain or snow. Pandas eat flowers, grass and sometimes small animals and honey. But bamboo, a tall, woody grass, is their main food. A giant panda needs 20 kilos of bamboo a day, and must eat for ten hours. Three kinds of bamboo are strong enough to grow in the giant panda's forests, but these bamboos have a strange life-cycle. The plant grows for almost 100 years. Then suddenly it flowers, drops its seeds and dies. The seeds grow very slowly, so, for a long time, there is no bamboo. And all the bamboos in one place flower – and die – at the same time.

In ancient times bamboo forests covered much of China. When the bamboo died in one place the pandas could move to another area for food. But people cut down the forests and the pandas had to climb higher into the mountains, into small 'islands' of bamboo forest. Now when the bamboo dies there is nowhere for the pandas to go, so they too die. We know that 140 pandas died in 1975/76 when the bamboo suddenly flowered. Experts think there are only 400–1,000 wild pandas alive today.

Since 1939 the Chinese government has been trying to help the panda. No-one may cut down bamboo forests or catch pandas. There are schemes to teach country people about the panda, and, since 1974, there have been ten special nature reserves for pandas. In the most famous of these, Wolong, a team of

Bamboo is the giant panda's main food.

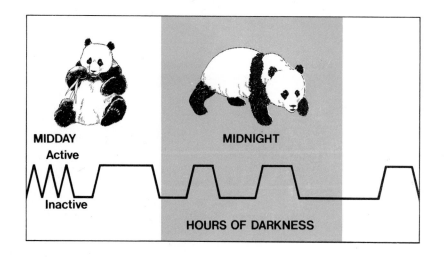

MIDDAY
Active
Inactive

MIDNIGHT

HOURS OF DARKNESS

One-day activity cycle of a panda in the wild.

scientists are making a special study of the panda, its way of life, home and food. They are also trying to breed pandas in new zoos, and to grow different kinds of bamboo for the reserves.

Professor Hu Chin Chu of Sichuan leads the Chinese team, and Dr George Schaller of New York comes from the World Wildlife Fund. Together they are studying the wild pandas in Wolong Reserve. First they caught five pandas and put radio collars on them. These collars send out radio signals, so the scientists can follow the pandas and find the answers to many questions. How far do pandas travel? Do they move with the seasons? How often do they rest? Do they sleep by day or night? The scientists have learnt that pandas are rather quiet animals who like to live alone. And they have found life in panda country cold and difficult. For days on end they never see a panda, but there have been some exciting moments.

One day George Schaller found some strange tracks in the snow. He waited and watched. A panda appeared at the top of the hill and slid down the snow. When it got to the bottom it walked up to the top and slid down again. So pandas have their own kind of

winter sports. Once the scientists were in danger from a panda. In late October Professor Hu and Dr Schaller were tracking a female panda, Zhen-Zhen, when she suddenly turned and ran angrily towards them. Schaller jumped into a tree and Professor Hu ran back down the hill. Why had Zhen-Zhen attacked them? After a careful search they found out her secret – she had a baby panda, about one and a half months old.

Baby pandas are our hope for the future of this strange, beautiful animal. Perhaps the most exciting piece of wildlife news in 1982 came from Madrid Zoo. Shao-Shao, their female panda, had twins. The father was Chia-Chia from London Zoo, and officials in both countries could hardly believe their success. Shao-Shao's twins were the first live panda births outside China. One baby died, but the other lives, a wonderful example of international teamwork in science. When people from different countries work together in this way then there is hope, not just for animals in danger, but for the whole world. Man, the most dangerous animal of all, has started to work *with* Nature. But has the killing stopped in time? Are we doing enough to save the panda, the elephant and the tiger?

Notes
drought a long time without any rain.
breed to produce baby animals.

warden a warden looks after wild animals in a game park and fights poachers.

Exercises

A Before you read
1 Look at the photos on p. 36–39. Have you seen any of these animals alive in (a) a zoo (b) a nature reserve (c) a game park?
2 How is man a danger to animals? How can people save wild animals? Make two lists of your ideas. Then see if your ideas are in the text.

B Read for ideas
1 Is man the *only* danger to wild animals?
2 What three things must balance but often do not?
3 Why do people kill wild animals? Are there any good reasons?
4 Complete these notes on cause and effect.

> **India:** People cut down trees – forests disappear. *Result:* . . . . .
> **Uganda 1960s:** Human population grew – no room for elephants. *Result:* . . . . .
> **Uganda 1970s:** War in Uganda. High price of ivory. *Result:* . . . . .
> **Zimbabwe:** Terrible drought – not enough food for elephants. *Result:* . . . . .
> **China:** Pandas eat special bamboo. Bamboo suddenly died. *Result:* . . . . .

5 Here are six ways to help wild life. Divide them into (1) what governments can do (2) what scientists can do.
   (a) control killing and sale of skins, etc.
   (b) try to breed animals in zoos.
   (c) educate people about wildlife.
   (d) make special reserves and game parks.
   (e) study wild animals' life and food.
   (f) look for new kinds of food.
   Mark each way with *A* for Africa and/or *C* for China.

C What do you think?
1 Why is it important to save rare animals?
2 What can (a) international organisations (b) ordinary people do to save wild life?

D Read for detail
1 Read p. 36–38 and study the maps on p. 37.
   (a) About how many elephants were outside Kabalega park in 1966? In which part of the park are most of the elephants?
   (b) By 1976 the elephant population had dropped to about (a) 8000 (b) 1700 (c) 200. Why?
   (c) Where were the last few elephants in 1980?

2 Study the diagram on p. 40. Are these statements true or false?
   (a) Pandas are active in the evenings.
   (b) Pandas sleep all night.
   (c) Pandas rest in the middle of the day.
   (d) Pandas walk on their back legs.
   (e) Pandas bring food up to their mouths.

E Read for language
1 Match the idioms with the meanings below.
   (a) to find a market
   (b) to sell on the open market
   (c) it does not pay

   (1) you do not get much money from it
   (2) to find a person who will buy things you want to sell
   (3) to sell goods officially

2 (a) Complete this description of a panda's life with words for time.
      'Pandas are active in the . . . and again in the . . . . They sleep or rest in the middle of the . . . and in the middle of the . . . . A panda must eat 20 kg of bamboo a . . . , so it eats for ten . . . . In . . . pandas live high up on the mountains but in . . . they move down to find food.'
   (b) Describe a domestic animal's life.

F Join the World Wildlife Fund.
For information write to:
   World Wildlife Fund,
   11–13 Ockford Road,
   Godalming,
   Surrey GU7 1QU, U.K.

41

7 Run for your life

How healthy are you? Is your body in good shape? And are you happy?
Doctors and sports experts have found that many people are fat, unfit
and unhappy. But they've also found an answer: running. Ordinary
people, doctors, scientists and sports experts all agree. Running is good
for you and running is fun. If *you* don't run, why not start? Will
running be right for you? Try our questionnaire and find out.

		Yes	No
1	Are you five or more kilograms overweight?	☐	☐
2	Do you smoke?	☐	☐
3	Would you like to lose weight?	☐	☐
4	Have you ever worried about your heart?	☐	☐
5	Would you like to reduce the danger of a heart attack?	☐	☐
6	Do you feel you're not in the shape you once were?	☐	☐
7	Would you like to get back into shape?	☐	☐
8	Would you like to feel better about the amount of exercise you're getting?	☐	☐
9	Would you like to sleep more deeply?	☐	☐
10	Would you like to need less sleep?	☐	☐
11	Would you like to feel calmer?	☐	☐
12	Do you like evenings by yourself or perhaps with one close friend better than large parties?	☐	☐
13	At large parties do you ever feel like a stranger?	☐	☐
14	Are you brave enough to be a little different from other people?	☐	☐
15	Are you usually happy when you're alone?	☐	☐

Yes to 12 or more.	Running is right for you.
Yes to 8–11.	You will enjoy running.
Yes to 5–8.	You may enjoy running – or you may not.
Yes to 0–4.	You won't enjoy running.

Running is good for you, and running is fun.

Run for fun

Once a year thousands of people forget about the Sunday papers and Sunday lunch and go to Hyde Park for the Sunday Times National Fun Run. They come with their friends, in families, or in teams from their place of work. What kind of people are they, the Fun Runners? Why do they do it?

'Running is good for you,' says Bobbi Randall, mother of six and a Fun Runner. 'I'm the only fat person in my family,' she wrote when she asked to join the Fun Runner scheme. 'I sit down all day in my job, and my hobbies – reading and knitting – don't give me any exercise. I just can't lose weight. Perhaps I've been too fat for too long?' At 47 Bobbi weighed 80 kg, and tests on her heart and lungs showed she was very unfit. She started to jog. After eleven weeks she had lost only $2\frac{1}{2}$ kg, but she was a lot fitter. Ten weeks later she had lost another $2\frac{1}{2}$ kg, and her fitness level was 'good'. She now jogs 5 km every day, easily.

'Running is good for your figure,' says Teresa Malinowska, aged 27. She is a tall woman, but was overweight at 70 kg. She also smoked five cigarettes a day. When Teresa started to jog she began to eat more – fruit and vegetables, bread and cheese, and sweets! But she didn't put on weight. Her body started to burn up food faster and she lost 1 kg. Tests showed she had lost 3 kg of fat and put on 2 kg of muscle. And she was a better shape.

'Running has changed my life,' says Dave Dyke, a 34-year-old painter and decorator. He hated exercise at school and had taken none since the age of 16. For years he used to smoke 20 cigarettes a day. His first fitness tests in April showed a result below average. So he started to train. At first he worked too hard and hurt himself. That was a mistake, but after a month he found the right programme and soon became fitter. By July he had lost 20% of his body fat and had moved up to fitness level 1, 'excellent'.

'Running is good for my nerves,' says Rodney Lewis, a taxi-driver. 'I used to scream at all those other stupid drivers, but now I stay calm.' Debbie Hoyle, a young mother, agrees. 'I love my two babies but I do need a rest from them. Running is good for my health, my

43

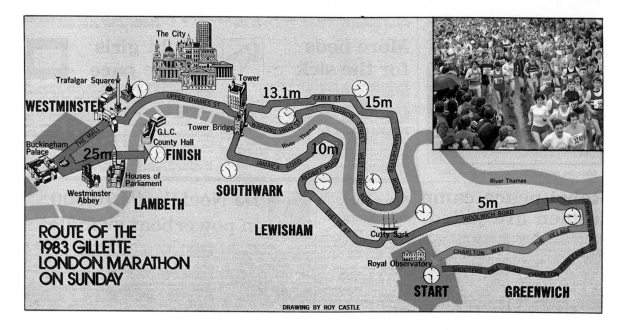

ROUTE OF THE
1983 GILLETTE
LONDON MARATHON
ON SUNDAY

The City
Trafalgar Square
Tower
13.1m
CABLE ST
15m
UPPER THAMES ST
NARROW
WESTMINSTER
Tower Bridge
WAPPING HIGH ST
River Thames
10m
Buckingham
Palace
THE MALL
G.L.C.
County Hall
FINISH
25m
JAMAICA ROAD
REDRIFF ROAD
Houses of
Parliament
Westminster
Abbey
SOUTHWARK
LEWISHAM
EVELYN ST
Cutty Sark
Royal Observatory
River Thames
5m
WOOLWICH ROAD
THE VILLAGE
JOHN WILSON ST
LAMBETH
CHARLTON WAY
CHARLTON PARK LANE
SHOOTERS HILL ROAD
START
GREENWICH

DRAWING BY ROY CASTLE

figure and my nerves. It's just the right kind of exercise for me.'

'I run to save my life,' says John Routledge, a businessman in his 50s. He has already 'died' once, after a heart attack a year ago. The hospital just saved his life, but when he got home, John decided to get fit, fast. He started to eat and drink less, and to jog. He quickly lost 9 kg and then joined the Getting in Shape programme for the National Fun Run. There are different kinds of exercise in the programme – walking, jogging, running, swimming or cycling – but they all help the unfit. You don't need drugs or doctors. You can do it yourself. But remember. You must train for the Fun Run, and you must start slowly.

Run a marathon

If you think the marathon is a difficult race, for Olympic athletes only, you're wrong. Thousands of ordinary people are now running marathons, in New York, Paris, Tokyo, Sydney and London. Marathons are sports festivals for men and women of all ages, for people of all shapes and sizes, for professional athletes and fun-runners. But one thing is the same: they all train for a year first.

Monica Fisher is a 50-year-old housewife but she decided to run in the London Marathon. She used to leave her house at six in the morning. 'I didn't want the neighbours to see me and laugh.' She finished the marathon in five hours. The men in her family were rude about her time. 'Five hours? I could run a marathon in that time.' 'If *you* can do it, anybody can.' 'Grr,' says Monica. 'Did they get up early to train? Could they get to the *start* of a marathon? I've made the decision to run again this year. That's the hard part. And I shall only try to beat one thing – the bus at the back of the race that picks up the drop-outs.'

The oldest runner in 1982 was 70-year-old George Brennan from Scotland. He started to run at the age of 65, after many years as a hall porter in an Edinburgh hotel. Five years later he completed the London Marathon in under four hours – a wonderful time for a man of his age. He writes, 'Perhaps you would like to know about my progress since then. I continued to train and entered both

the Edinburgh and Glasgow Marathons. I finished the first – in terrible weather – in 3 hrs 45 mins. I finished at Glasgow in 3 hrs 36 mins! That's not bad for a 70-year-old, is it? But Kathleen, my wife, has asked me to stop now. I'll just run for fun, not in the marathon.'

Cheryl Page has already run in four marathons, one in Germany, two in Britain and one in San Francisco, USA. She finished in a splendid time of 4 hrs 10 mins in front of TV cameras. What's special about Cheryl? She ran her first marathon at the age of 10, and her fourth at 11! She's the youngest marathon runner in the world.

Her father, Major Brian Page, explains. 'We were living in Germany and often used to go for long family walks in Berlin. Cheryl always came with us and at the age of 6 she completed a 24-km walk easily. Then I started to train at a Sports Centre and Cheryl came

The Marathon – a sports festival for all.

with me. We both started to run, and Cheryl was very good at it. Soon she could run 8 km with no difficulty. So, we decided to enter a 25-km race. I had run 20 km and Cheryl had done 13 km, so we agreed to run for the first 13 km and walk for the second half of the way. But when we got to 13 km Cheryl would not slow down. At 23 km I said, 'Look, Cheryl, I'm very tired. I'm going to walk now.'

Cheryl takes up the story 'Poor old Dad,' she says. 'I wouldn't stop. There were only 2 km to go. Why give up just before the end?' Soon Cheryl wanted to try a really long run, the marathon. For her first marathon she ran hand-in-hand with her father, and they took 4 hrs 53 mins. 'I was a bit tired the next day,' she says. On her third marathon Cheryl let go of her father's hand and waved goodbye. She finished 20 minutes before him. What will she do next?

Follow the marathon – from an armchair

'Running a marathon is the worst thing in the world,' my friends tell me. 'But finishing a marathon is the best.'

I don't try. I just watch marathons on TV and read the stories in the newspapers. That's my idea of fun. Did you know that there was a pantomime horse in the London Marathon? The front legs finished in 3 hrs 28 mins 56 secs, but the back legs arrived a full second later. Did you hear about the woman in the New York Marathon who caught a train for part of the way? Or the man in Budapest who hitched a lift in a car? And watch out for Roger Bourban, the fastest waiter in the West.

Bourban comes from a Swiss family, but works in California. When he runs he always carries an *open* bottle of mineral water on a tray. 'I'm telling people that mineral water is good for them,' he says. 'And I'm showing the world that waiters are great artists.'

If you're fat and unfit, don't worry about it. Worry is bad for you. While other people get up early to jog, stay in bed and rest. Remember – there are many roads to a healthy, happy life. I believe in good food, plenty of sleep, comfortable armchairs and nice friends. Run a marathon? Run for fun? Never.

Notes

The Sunday Times a Sunday newspaper.
Hyde Park a large park in the centre of London.
marathon a race of 26 miles, 385 yards or 42,195 km.
       (Best times: women 2 hrs 25 mins 29 secs
       men 2 hrs 8 mins 13 secs)

Exercises

A Before you read

1 Look at the photos on p. 44 and 45. What are all the people doing? What kind of people are they? Would you join them?

2 Do you know these words for parts of the body: *heart   lungs   muscle   fat   nerves*? Check with your teacher or a dictionary.

B Read for ideas

1 Put the main points of the unit in the right order.
   (a) Many people are unhealthy and unhappy.
   (b) Thousands of people join in Fun Runs.
   (c) It's important to train first.
   (d) People of all ages also run marathons.
   (e) They follow programmes for Getting-in-Shape before the Fun Run.
   (f) But some people don't enjoy running. They believe in good food and rest.
   (g) Running can help them. It's good for the body and it's fun.

2 What is the purpose of the text on p. 46?
   (a) to make the reader laugh
   (b) to say running is dangerous
   (c) to persuade people to watch TV more

C Read for inference

Find evidence in the text to support your answers to these questions:
(a) Is smoking good for you?
(b) What usually happens if you eat sweets?
(c) Does everyone finish the marathon?

(d) In which city did George run a marathon in 3 hrs 45 mins?
(e) Where did Cheryl run her first marathon?
(f) Where did Cheryl run a marathon in 4 hrs 10 mins?
(g) Are marathons run in sports centres?

D What do you think?

1 Is it a good idea for very old or very young people to run marathons?

2 Which of these two sayings do you agree with? Why?
'Remember, if you feel the need for exercise, wait for the feeling to go away.'
'A journey of 1,000 miles begins with a single step.'

E Read for languge

1 Make nouns from these verbs:
   run   jog   knit   read   walk   swim   cycle
   Example: run → running

2 Write these abbreviations out in full:
   (a) 70 kg   (b) $2\frac{1}{2}$ kg   (c) 24 km   (d) 3 hrs 28 mins 56 secs

3 Persuade someone to take up running. Complete these sentences with the right form of the word in brackets.
   'Why don't you take up (run)? You'll sleep (deeply) and feel (calm). You'll burn up food (fast) and lose (weight). You'll soon be much (fit) and in (good) shape. And you'll be (happy) too.'

Get in shape!
Compare the different kinds of exercise, and choose the right one for you.

	Calories/hour	Stamina	Strength	Part best for	Muscle
Running	600	• • • •	• •	legs/heart	•
Walking	240	• •	•	legs	•
Cycling	400	• • • •	• • •	legs/heart	• •
Swimming	600	• • • •	• • • •	all over	• • •
Tennis	390	• • •	• •	all over	• •

• no real effect
• • good effect
• • • very good effect
• • • • excellent effect

8 Knits in fashion

Knitting is news, and new hand-knits are high fashion. Sweaters and jerseys are now part of every smart person's wardrobe. Season after season fashion buyers come from all over the world to buy the best of British knitting, the traditional arans and fair-isles or the new designer knits. *Artwork* is one of the leading makers of modern hand-knits. This company, with its office and studio in south-east London, was the idea of two young design students from the Central School of Art, Jane Foster and Patrick Gottelier. 'We wanted to bring modern fashion into the traditional art of hand-knitting,' they explain, 'so we decided to design our first collection.'

That was in 1977 and now they bring out a new collection twice a year, summer and winter. 'We find ideas in all kinds of places,' says Jane. 'One year it was the pattern of bricks in a wall. Other years we've come back from holidays in Italy and Japan with lots of ideas for colour and patterns.'

'Knitting from the past gives us ideas too,' says Patrick. 'One Christmas our designs looked back to the Middle Ages. Another collection had a lot of bead-work in it. You can see eighteenth-century examples in museums like the Victoria and Albert.

'But you can't just copy ideas from the past,' Jane adds. 'You have to think of designs that will be part of modern fashion.'

Who knits all the sweaters? 'We translate our designs into patterns that our knitters can easily follow,' says Patrick. 'My mother found our first knitters for us, and now we have a large team.'

Who buys them? 'All kinds of people, and they come back each year for more. We're always busy.'

Says one happy customer, 'You know, I don't often wear my Artwork sweaters. I collect them – a new one every season. They

Jane and Patrick in Artwork sweaters.

really are works of art, and I want to save them for my grandchildren.'

Other people choose traditional British knits. The guernseys, arans and fair-isle sweaters now in fashion all have their roots in the life of the past – in the life of sea folk. You find the best of British folk-knitting in the small islands round the coast. The word 'jersey' for knitted clothes comes from one of the Channel Islands. Sailors and fishermen from Jersey wore shirts knitted in coloured wool. When they visited different ports, other people copied their idea for warm clothing and gave it the name of the sailors' island.

One special kind of sailor's jersey comes from the next-door island of Guernsey. Mothers, wives and girl-friends knitted guernseys for their men. They always used thick, dark blue wool, and they knitted special designs on the front and round the chest and shoulders. One favourite design was 'marriage lines'. Its lines go up and down to remind people of the good and bad times in life. The women also designed their own

patterns or worked the names of their true loves into their guernseys. The men had to be able to work easily on the boats, so the sleeves were always rather short. All real guernseys are thick and warm, and keep out both the wind and sea water.

The isles of Aran, off the West coast of Ireland, are famous for their sweaters. For a true Aran you must use thick cream or Bainin wool (Bainin is the Irish word for white) and different traditional stitches and patterns.

(right) This picture from 9th century Ireland shows St. Daniel in his winter clothes, knitted Aran stockings and a Bainin sweater.

The Irish are Celts and you find the same designs in Aran knitwear and ancient Celtic metalwork, stonework and jewellery: crosses, circles and diamonds. Aran designs have special meanings. A diamond will bring money, but the tree of life pattern is the sign of a long life and many strong sons. Some patterns come from Christianity, the cross and the three-in-one 'trinity' stitch. Others remind us of the daily life of sailors and fishermen. The cable patterns mean ropes and the zig-zags are the paths down to the sea. Different families and different villages had their own special designs. When a sailor drowned, people always knew his name and his home village. The patterns on his sweater told them.

In the north of Scotland lie the Shetland Islands, home of the famous Shetland sweater. The people of Shetland came from Norway in the ninth and tenth centuries, so Shetland designs are part of the Scandinavian tradition of knitting – a rich mixture of different shapes: circles, squares, triangles and diamonds. Shetland designs use the colours of natural wool, white, grey, brown or black, with perhaps one bright colour in the pattern round the neck.

Fair-isle sweaters, from an island between the Shetlands and the coast of Scotland, are full of pattern and colour. The designs first came to the island with Viking sailors. They had travelled to North Africa and copied the patterns they saw there. The islanders use vegetables and fruit to colour their wool, and then knit sweaters with bands of different patterns. Another story tells us that in 1588 a ship from the Spanish Armada sank in a storm near Fair Isle. Some of the sailors reached dry land and married the girls on Fair Isle. Their wives learned to knit the new Spanish patterns, and then taught their children and

⬤	1st colour	⊡	4th colour
▲	2nd colour	◼	5th colour
☐	3rd colour		

50

This picture from the 18th century shows a Yorkshire village. Man or woman, young or old, everyone is knitting. People knitted in the village square, they knitted on the way to market, and young lovers took their knitting with them on evening walks.

grandchildren. To this day one shape is called 'the Armada Cross' and others have a Christian meaning, 'the sacred heart' or 'the star of life'. Fair-isle sweaters now come from factories all over the world, but the best are still hand-knits from Scotland.

Great British knits are part of the world family of folk knitting, like sweaters from Scandinavia, caps from Peru or socks from Afghanistan. They all have their roots in an ancient craft with an interesting history. Today most people think knitting is women's work, but it used to be a man's job. When knitting began, about the fourth or fifth century B.C. in the Middle East, the women spun the wool from the sheep and the men knitted it into cloth. The art of knitting then spread from the Arab world into Europe and Asia. Pictures from many different countries show people in knitted hats, shirts, and stockings, with knitted carpets in their homes. In the sixteenth century there was a busy hand-knitting industry in Europe, and in England

A famous picture from the Landes area of France. It shows a shepherd on stilts. He is watching his sheep and knitting a sock at the same time.

Queen Elizabeth I made a law to help the national industry.

'Every person above the age of seven shall wear upon Sundays or public holidays … upon their heads a cap of wool, knitted in England.'

Then, in 1589, William Lee of Nottingham invented the knitting machine and the hand-knitting industry slowly died. But the folk craft of knitting lived on in many parts of the world. Shepherds and fishermen continued to knit their own socks and sweaters, and mothers, aunts and grandmothers knitted clothes for their families. Today knitting is a favourite hobby, and everyone is wearing hand-knits. You can choose from folk jerseys or designer knits. Buy an expensive sweater from a shop, or knit one for half the price at home. You'll be in fashion, and you'll be part of a great tradition too.

(above) In fashion – and part of a great tradition, too.
(left) In the cold mountains of Peru, children wear bright knitted caps and sweaters.

Notes
Vikings a people from Scandinavia in the 8th–10th
      centuries.
Armada ships from Spain which fought against
      England in 1588.
beads very small balls with a hole through the centre,
      often brightly coloured.

Exercises

A Before you read

1 Mark these statements true or false.
   - (a) Knitting began in North Europe.
   - (b) Knitting has always been a woman's job.
   - (c) London is a centre of knitting fashion.
   - (d) Smart people wear traditional folk knits.
2 Read the text and check your answers.

B Read for ideas

1 Copy this diagram of the text. Put one topic in each of the boxes:
   (a) world of folk knitting (b) modern designer knits (c) a short history of knitting (d) traditional British knits
   Write place names on the lines (. . . . . . .)

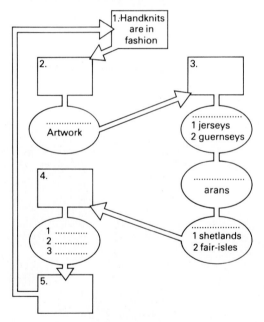

2 Where do 'Artwork' designs come from?
3 Who knit 'Artwork' sweaters?
4 What kind of people needed thick jerseys?
5 Why are Spanish designs like Scottish ones?

C Read for detail

1 Label this guernsey:
   neck   shoulders   front
   back   sleeves   chest

2 Match the sweaters and colours:

Aran	bright colours
Guernsey	natural colours
Shetland	cream
Fair Isle	dark blue

3 Which sweaters have patterns (a) in colour (b) in stitches?
4 Which sweater has short sleeves? Why?
5 Find three examples of folk designs and explain their meaning.

D Talk about knitting

1 Do you wear handknits? If so, do you knit them yourself, does someone knit them for you, or do you buy them?
2 Which of the sweaters on p. 48–52 do you like best? Why?

E Read for language

1 What does 'wardrobe' (line 3) mean? Is it 1, 2 or 3 in this dictionary entry?

   war·drobe /ˈwɔːdrəʊb‖ˈwɔr-/ *n* **1** a room, cupboard, or large upright box, with a door, in which one hangs up clothes —see picture at BEDROOM **2** a collection of clothes (esp. of one person or for one activity): *a new summer wardrobe* **3** a collection of special historical clothes (COSTUMEs) and ornaments to be worn in a theatre

2 What are the names for these shapes?

3 What is the difference between a job, an industry and a hobby?
4 Write a description of a person you know well: colour of hair and eyes, figure, job, hobbies, style of clothes. Then describe a sweater to suit that person.

F Know the wash code

What do these symbols on a sweater mean?

(*Answers: See p. 96*)

9 BACK TO THE BIKE

Private car or public transport – it's the same thing. Travelling to work gets more difficult and more expensive every year. Ordinary people can do nothing about the world price of petrol, or a national rise in fares. They have to get to work, so they have to pay. Or do they? People are looking for cheaper kinds of transport, and they have found one – from the past. They are going back to the bike.

Children often go to school by bike and students cycle to class. But now businessmen are going to the office by bike. 'The bicycle,' says Mr Brown, 'is a businessman's dream. It's easy to make and it's cheap. You can buy

Cycling is cheap, healthy – and fun!

thirty bikes for the price of one small car. A bike doesn't use expensive fuel, like petrol, but runs on manpower. You don't have large bills for repairs – a child of ten can learn to look after a bicycle. And most bikes will last a lifetime.'

'Cycling is good for you,' adds Dr Williams. Every day he cycles to St. Bartholomew's Hospital in the centre of London. 'Drivers sit in traffic jams and get angry. That's bad for the heart. Then they can't find a place to park and get angrier! And many of them get fat too. Twentieth-century people don't get enough exercise, so I tell all my patients to buy a bike. If you cycle to work you save petrol, save money and save your health. And you often save time too. In London, it's quicker to travel by bike than by bus!'

Bikes by the barges of Amsterdam.

Cycling is clean, quiet, cheap and healthy. And it can also be fun. Cycle to work all week and go for a cycle ride in the country at the weekend. Or go on a cycling holiday.

A bike in every port

Journalist Adam Hopkins went on holiday round North Europe. He decided to try out a bike in every port. 'At Trondheim in Norway I found a bicycle shop and hired a bike for the day. They didn't ask me for a deposit. I thought this was strange, but then I remembered that Norway is all mountains. Inside the town itself there are some very steep hills. I tried to cycle up to the Folk Museum, but had to push the bike for the last half hour! Lots of Norwegians cycle in Trondheim, and they are all very fit.

'In Amsterdam I had to pay a deposit of £12, but the cost of hire was only £1.40 a day. Amsterdam is *the* city for cyclists. They rule the roads. There are special cycle-ways in the city centre, and special traffic lights. They show a little bicycle in red, orange or green, for stop, wait and go. I had some difficulty with the brakes on a Dutch bicycle. When you want to stop, you must pedal backwards. But I always forgot. Then there are the trams. Cycle wheels can easily stick in a tramline if you're not careful, and Dutch trams move fast. Out of the centre of town I rode along by the canals, and enjoyed every minute of it ... the long lines of beautiful houses, the flowers on the barges.

'It's best to see most of Copenhagen on foot, but I tried out a bike there too. Don't cycle after too many glasses of Danish lager! That was my worst mistake. I'm thinking about a two-week cycling holiday in Holland or Denmark next summer. The people are friendly, the food is good, and there aren't any hills. What more can a cyclist want?'

Try before you buy

If you haven't ridden a bike for years, don't buy one – yet. Borrow one from a friend, or hire one from a shop. You can hire a bike quite cheaply in many big towns. But hire or buy, you must always check a bicycle properly. If it's all right, then you can go for a ride.

Cycle checklist	Yes	No
	☐	☐
1 Sit on the bike. Is the saddle the right height for you? Can you touch the ground with the ball of your foot?		
	☐	☐
2 Spin the wheels round. Do they spin easily and evenly?	☐	☐
3 Put the brakes on hard. Push the bike. Can you move it at all?	☐	☐
4 Brake gently. Do the wheels stop smoothly? Are the brake blocks just touching the wheel rim?		
	☐	☐
5 Raise the wheel off the ground and spin the pedals. Do they run silently?		
	☐	☐
6 Shake the whole bicycle. Is there a noise anywhere?	☐	☐
7 Check all the nuts and bolts. Are any of them loose?	☐	☐
8 Check the tyres. Are they both hard?		

The right answers are : 1 Yes 2 Yes 3 No 4 Yes 5 Yes 6 No 7 No 8 Yes

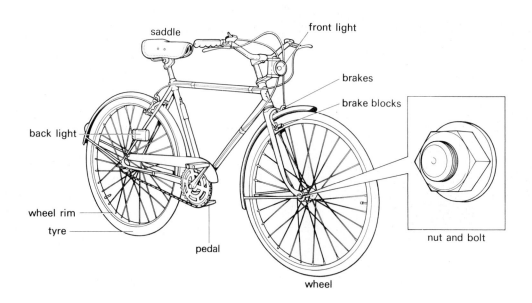

saddle front light brakes brake blocks back light wheel rim tyre pedal nut and bolt wheel

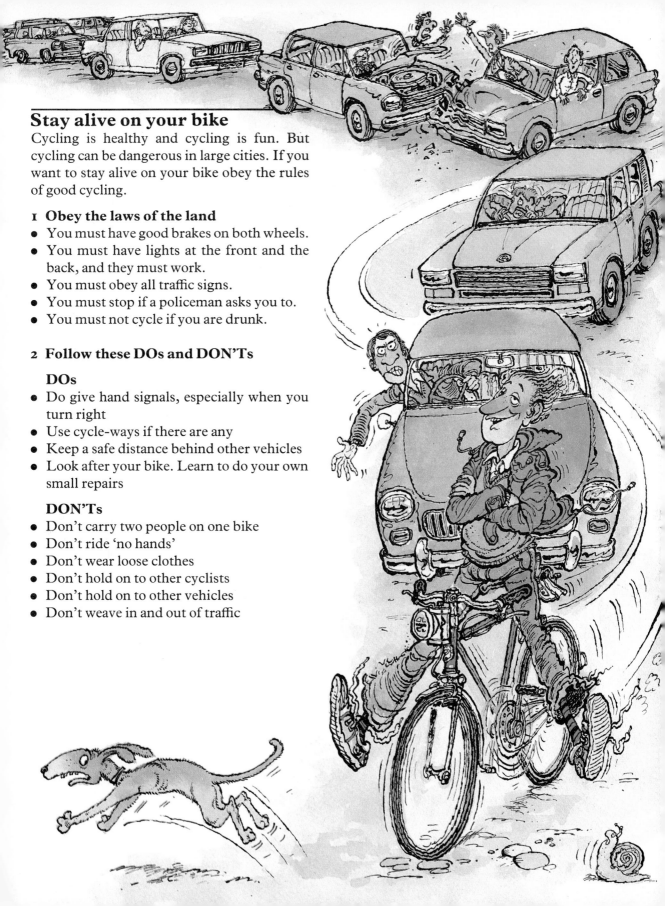

Stay alive on your bike

Cycling is healthy and cycling is fun. But cycling can be dangerous in large cities. If you want to stay alive on your bike obey the rules of good cycling.

1 Obey the laws of the land

- You must have good brakes on both wheels.
- You must have lights at the front and the back, and they must work.
- You must obey all traffic signs.
- You must stop if a policeman asks you to.
- You must not cycle if you are drunk.

2 Follow these DOs and DON'Ts

DOs

- Do give hand signals, especially when you turn right
- Use cycle-ways if there are any
- Keep a safe distance behind other vehicles
- Look after your bike. Learn to do your own small repairs

DON'Ts

- Don't carry two people on one bike
- Don't ride 'no hands'
- Don't wear loose clothes
- Don't hold on to other cyclists
- Don't hold on to other vehicles
- Don't weave in and out of traffic

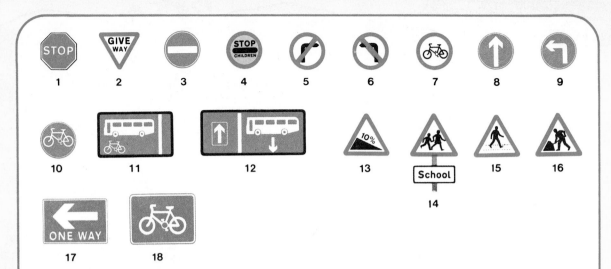

Know your traffic signs.

a) You may use the bus lane
b) Road works
c) One way street
d) Route for pedal cyclists
e) No right turn
f) Give way to traffic off major road
g) Turn left ahead
h) Steep hill
i) No cycling

j) You may not use the bus lane
k) Pedestrian crossing
l) Stop and give way
m) School crossing
n) No entry
o) No left turn
p) Children going to and from school
q) Route to be used by pedal cyclists only
r) Ahead only

Journey's End

Mr Michael Murphy, aged 22, from Stevenage in Hertfordshire, left England in 1975. He had decided to cycle round the world. For two whole years he met with many dangers and difficulties. In Yugoslavia thieves stole his clothes. In the mountains of the Khyber Pass, people threw stones at him. And he nearly froze to death in a snow-storm in Finland. He flew back to England in April 1977. He had cycled 25,000 miles round the world and now had only 40 miles left, from Heathrow Airport to Hertfordshire. He waited in the Customs Hall for his bike. At last it appeared – in pieces. How did Mr Murphy get home? By train.

Exercises

A Before you read
Study this graph.

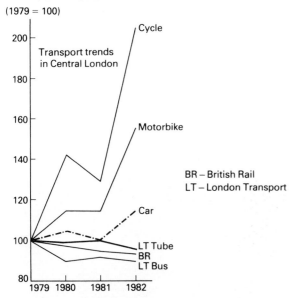

(1979 = 100)

Transport trends in Central London

BR – British Rail
LT – London Transport

1 In which year were there cheap fares on public transport: buses and tube?
2 Compare the information in the graph with the ideas in the first part of the text.

B Read for ideas
1 For each point *against* the car find one *for* the bicycle.

against cars	for bikes
expensive to buy expensive to run: petrol, repairs traffic jams: so slow parking problems unhealthy for drivers	

2 Complete this chart to compare Hopkins' holiday with Murphy's tour.

1 Hopkins' difficulties	2 Murphy's dangers
Norway .... Holland .... Denmark	Yugoslavia .... Khyber Pass .... Finland ....

3 What is important for a good cycling holiday?

C Read for detail
1 Is it safe to ride this bike? See p. 56.
   When you put the brakes on hard you can still push the bike forward.
   When you brake gently the brake blocks don't touch the wheel rim.
   When you shake the bicycle there is a strange noise.
   The front tyre is soft.

2 Do you know your traffic signs? Study the signs on p. 58 and match the words to the signs.
   Example: 18 (a)

D State your case
1 Make a case *against* cycling in cities.
2 Argue *for* and *against* this statement:
   'Keep private cars out of city centres.'

E Read for language
1 Divide the words for vehicles in the text into two groups: public and private transport.

2 Find the comparative forms of these adjectives:
   cheap   angry   quick   difficult   expensive

3 How good is your road sense? Read p. 57.
   Copy the rules and write a reason for each.
   Example **Rule:** You must have good brakes on both wheels. **Reason:** You may have to stop suddenly.
   Compare your ideas with other students.

F Class survey
1 How do people travel to work? Complete this chart with the right numbers.

Bus	Tube	Car	Bike	Train	On foot

2 Compare people's journeys to work: type of transport, cost, distance, time.

10 Holidays with a difference

Why go on holiday to eat, sleep and lie in the sun? Why drive hundreds of miles to look at old buildings or famous pictures? Try a holiday with a difference. Do something. Learn something. Take up a new sport or paint your own pictures. A change is as good as a rest. And the best kind of play is work. Use your body, use your mind, and really enjoy your holiday. There are hundreds of holidays with a difference, and they don't cost a fortune.

Learn to cook the French way – in France

The French are famous for their good food – and for teaching foreigners to cook it! French chefs followed Napoleon and his army round Europe, and since then the best restaurants in many cities have been French. Some people say, 'If you can read, you can cook!' But that is not quite true. You will cook French recipes much better if you can watch a French chef at work.

If you'd like to learn the art of French cooking, try a holiday cookery course this year. There are two courses a year in Dieppe, one in the spring and the other in the autumn. Each course lasts six days and is held in one of Dieppe's best hotels. You spend the mornings in the hotel kitchens with a French master chef. He cooks one of the great dishes of France and explains its special secrets. It doesn't matter if you don't speak French. All the recipes are translated into English.

In the afternoons there are visits to places of interest, especially to lovers of good food and drink. You can visit a cheese farm, and buy one of Normandy's famous cheeses as a souvenir. You will go to the distillery at Fécamp, and see the home of Benedictine liqueur. But the Benedictine monks will not teach you *their* secrets! If you want a quiet afternoon you can just drive into the pretty Normandy countryside and enjoy the fresh air. Or you can

A French master chef cooks great dishes of France.

60

explore the town of Dieppe, with its old castle and narrow streets.

At the end of the course you will receive the perfect souvenir – a book of French recipes. When you go home you will be able to cook some of the great dishes of France yourself. You will remember the secrets of French cooking, and will never forget your holiday with a difference.

Camembert – Normandy's famous cheese.

Take the Connemara trail

If you can ride, you would enjoy one of Willie Leahy's riding holidays. Forget city life, with its noise and traffic jams, and travel on horseback through the lovely Irish countryside. Take the Connemara trail from Galway to Clifden. Far away on the west coast of Ireland there are few people, few roads and hardly any cars. Instead you will find green valleys and quiet beaches, beautiful mountains and dangerous bogs. People come from all over the world to Connemara for the riding holiday of a lifetime.

Kurt Schmidt, a German businessman, says, 'This is the perfect holiday for me. I lead a very busy life, but I'm always in offices, taxis or planes. And I hardly ever get any exercise. A riding holiday gives me fresh air and exercise, and it gives my mind a rest too. After

On horseback through the Irish countryside.

Riders must look after their horses.

one day on a horse I forget all my business problems. And in Ireland I keep Irish time. Five minutes or half an hour – what does it matter? There's no hurry.'

On the first day, Willie chooses the right horse for each guest, and then the group sets out on the trail. You stay in a different hotel every two nights, and they are all first class. You may arrive wet from the Irish rain. You may ache all over after several hours on horseback. But you will soon feel better after a hot bath, a good meal and a glass of Irish coffee. And you will sleep like a child again.

Everything is done for you. Your luggage is taken to the next hotel. Lunch is booked at country inns, or you have a picnic in the open air. But riders must look after their horses themselves. You have to wash your horse, brush it and feed it each night. During the day you guide your horse along narrow paths or round the bogs – under that bright green grass there may be metres of black mud. You will cross rivers and climb up into the mountains.

A recipe for Irish Coffee

You will need : strong coffee   sugar
Irish whiskey   thick cream
a tall glass and a spoon

Pour some whiskey into the glass, and add a spoonful of sugar. Then pour strong coffee into the glass – but don't fill the glass to the top. Stir to mix the sugar in well. Now take the cream, and a spoon. Pour the cream into the glass over the back *of the spoon. Do this slowly and very carefully – the cream must stay on top of the coffee and whiskey. Wait a few minutes. Then drink your Irish coffee through the cream on top of the glass.*

You can ride along the sand and then take your horse for a swim in the sea. It's a wonderful open air holiday.

You must be a good rider for the Connemara Trail. It's not for beginners – and it's not cheap. It will cost you £250 for six days, including horse and full board. But you also have to pay to get to Galway. A riding holiday like this needs money and courage. But you will never forget it. If you do not want to say goodbye to your horse at the end of the holiday, then you can buy him. Willie will arrange to ship your horse to your home.

If you can't ride, you can always learn. There are many other holidays for beginners, with riding lessons every day.

Paint in the Pyrenees

Do you think only great artists can paint? Have you ever wanted to put brush to canvas? Now is the time to try.

On the walls of Mr and Mrs Johnson's London home, there are some beautiful paintings of Spain. Mary Johnson painted them herself, on holiday. 'I enjoyed art lessons when I was at school,' says Mary, 'but after that, I never seemed to have any time to paint. My job, and then my family, kept me very busy. I went back to work when the children started school. And that meant I was busier than ever. Then, two years ago, we heard of painting holidays. We joined a group of people – some professional artists, but most were amateurs – on a holiday visit to Berdun.

A valley in the Spanish Pyrenees. The light is wonderful for painting.

It's an old Spanish village on a hill rising from the valley of the river Aragon. It has marvellous views of the Spanish countryside – rolling lines of mountains to the south and the high Pyrenees to the north. The light is wonderful – so clear and bright. The fields really do look red in the evening sun, and I've tried to get the strange blue of the distant mountains. The tutor's helped me a lot, and I've also learned from the other people in the group.'

Were any of the paintings by her husband? Bill Johnson laughed. 'I'm afraid not,' he replied. 'But non-painters are welcome too. I enjoy the holidays as much as Mary. There's plenty for me to do. I've explored the little villages near Berdun, and visited many of the ancient churches and castles of Aragon.

There's a good library at the Painting School with books on the art and architecture of Spain. So I read in the evenings. We stay in one of the old houses in Berdun – it's modernised of course, with hot and cold water. The whole group eats in the village restaurant. The food is excellent and the wine is included, free, with all meals! It's a good life, and I keep fit by swimming in the river Veral, just below the village.'

Do they go every year? 'Last year was our fourth painting holiday at Berdun,' said Mary. 'So this year we're going to have a change.' 'Yes,' said Bill. 'We're going to Granada in the south of Spain – for a painting holiday. And I shall have plenty of time to see the Alhambra properly.'

A holiday without a difference

In 1971 Mr and Mrs Farmer of Margate in Kent travelled to Wales for their summer holidays. At the start of the week they joined a British Rail mystery tour. Early in the morning they got on the train. 'Perhaps we're going to see the Welsh mountains,' said Mrs Farmer. But the train took them back to Margate.

'I've been trying to get away from Margate all summer,' cried Mr Farmer angrily. 'And here we are, home again.'

Mr and Mrs Farmer refused to join the second part of the tour – a walk round Margate. Instead they went home for a nice cup of tea.

Notes
full board the cost of a room and all meals in a hotel, etc.

Exercises

A Before you read

1 What do you look for in a holiday? Tick the right boxes: (a) sun ☐ (b) good food ☐ (c) night life ☐ (d) a good rest ☐ (e) fresh air ☐ (f) interesting places to visit ☐ (g) beautiful countryside ☐ (h) the sea ☐

2 What kind of souvenirs do you bring back from your holidays?

B Read for ideas

1 The purpose of the first paragraph is to:
(a) inform (b) describe (c) explain
(d) persuade (e) instruct

2 Compare each of the holidays described with more traditional ones. Make lists in this form:

Holiday	Same	Different

3 What special souvenirs can people take home from the holidays described?
4 Which holiday was *not* for beginners?
5 Whose holiday went wrong?

C Read for detail

1 Find the names of:
(a) a town in Normandy
(b) a district in the West of Ireland
(c) an old Spanish village
(d) a beautiful Muslim palace in Spain
(e) a group of Christian men who never marry and make a special drink
(f) a famous French emperor

2 Find evidence for these statements:
(a) On a French cookery course you don't need to speak French or to cook yourself.
(b) Irish weather is not always perfect.
(c) You can have painting lessons on holiday.
(d) Wales is not a flat country.

D Talk about holidays

1 Describe a marvellous holiday you've had.
2 Have you ever been on a mystery tour?

E Read for language

1 What is the difference between (a) an inn (b) a hotel (c) a restaurant?
2 Make a list of all the words for
(a) buildings (b) the countryside
3 What are more ordinary words for:
(a) a tutor (b) a chef (c) a trail
4 Write a recipe for a traditional dish or drink from your country. Use the recipe for Irish coffee as a guide.

F Practical reading

1 Study these advertisements for holidays.

2 Choose a holiday for the Johnsons, Kurt Schmidt, yourself.
3 Write a letter to one of the holiday centres. Book a holiday for yourself.

11 How long will you live?

The oldest people in the world

Hundreds of people in the world are a hundred years old – or more. There are about two thousand centenarians in Britain alone, and certain parts of the world are famous for the long lives of their inhabitants: Georgia in the Soviet Union, the Vilacamba Valley in Ecuador, and the home of the Hunzas in the Himalayas. But the oldest person in the world is Japanese. In 1983 Mr Shigechiyo Izumi, aged 118, held first place in *The Guinness Book of Records*. He was born on June 29th, 1865 and beat the previous record on his 114th

Four centenarians from Georgia with a total age of 480!

Mr Izumi, the oldest man in the world.

birthday. Before Mr Izumi broke the record, the longest life was that of an American woman, Mrs Eveline Filkins. She lived for 113 years, 214 days, from 1815 to 1928. During her lifetime she saw the invention of the first camera, the first telephone, the first car, the first aeroplane and the first television. There are official papers to prove the date of birth of Mr Izumi and Mrs Filkins, but many other people claim to be as old or older.

The truth problem

In 1959, 224 men and 368 women told Soviet census officials that they were more than 120 years old. But no one could prove their real age. Were they telling the truth or not? One

(above) A Georgian couple after 100 years of marriage.

66

are remembering their parents' stories about the past. Everyone agrees that there are many very old people in Georgia, Ecuador and the Himalayas, but it is difficult to discover their true age.

The truth in a tooth?

Two scientists in California now think they can find out a person's real age. Jeffrey Bada and Patricia Masters do chemical tests on teeth. When we are born the amino acids in our teeth are in one form. Then, as we grow older, these amino acids change into a second form. Every year, one thousandth (1/1,000) of the amino acids change. So, by testing just one tooth and counting the number of amino acids in each form, Bada and Masters can work out a person's age. They tested a tooth from the body of an Eskimo woman who died 1,600 years ago. From the appearance of her body she was between 50 and 60 years old when she died. The tooth test put her age at 53. Then the Soviet Government sent them a tooth from an old woman in Georgia. The tooth test said she was 99. Her real age was 96. The Russians are now hoping to send more teeth, from the very old people without birth certificates. But there are problems. Some of the centenarians have lost all their teeth. The others want to keep their teeth until they drop out naturally. So the Soviet Government and the American scientists wait and hope.

old man in Azerbaijan lived to the age of 168. What was his secret? He could not add up, so he got his age wrong. A hundred years ago no one could read or write in mountain villages, so there were no lists of births and deaths. In one village, when the young men did not want to join the army, they added ten years to their real age. 'We are too old to fight,' they told the men from the city. For the rest of their lives they were ten years older than their real age. Fathers and sons often had the same name. A son saw his father's name on a list and said, 'That's me.' So, in one second, he added thirty years to his age. Some old people seem to know a lot about their country's history, but they are not remembering the past. They

The secret of a long life

Why do so many people live to a healthy old age in certain parts of the world? What is the secret of their long lives? Three things seem to be very important: fresh air, fresh food and a simple way of life. People work near their homes in the clean, mountain air instead of travelling long distances to work by bus, car or train. They do not sit all day in busy offices or factories, but work hard outdoors in the fields. They take more exercise and eat less food than people in the cities of the West. For years the Hunzas of the Himalayas did not need policemen, lawyers or doctors. There was no crime, no divorce and not much illness in their society. They were a happy, peaceful people, famous all over India for their long, healthy lives.

Sir Robert McCarrison, a doctor in the Indian Medical Service in the 1930s, decided to study the way of life of the healthy Hunzas, especially their diet. The Hunzas did not eat much food, and they only ate fresh food. They grew their own food in good soil and did not overcook it. Dr McCarrison compared the Hunza diet with that of another people who lived in the central lowlands. These people were fat, often ill and died young. They ate polished rice and a lot of sweet things. After comparing these two groups of people, Dr McCarrison decided to do some experiments with rats.

McCarrison's experiments

McCarrison took two groups of rats and fed them on different diets for 27 months. (This is the same as 50 years of human life.) He fed the first group on a diet of chapatis, fresh green beans, fresh fruit and a little meat. He gave the second group a diet of polished rice and sugar. The rats in the first group had no illnesses, lived to a good age and died naturally. They were happy, peaceful rats. But the other group quickly became ill, with skin and stomach trouble. They had difficulty with breathing, and many of them died young. They were unhappy rats, and often fought and killed each other.

McCarrison then gave the sick rats a Hunza diet. They soon grew better on the healthy diet, and lived to a good age. He also fed a

third group of rats on the diet of poor people in the North of England in the 1930s: white bread, jam and tea. These rats too quickly became fat, ill and unhappy. From these experiments comes the theory that the right diet leads to a long, happy and healthy life. In Ecuador and Georgia too, the people eat a diet low in calories, fresh from good soil, and they do not overcook their food. So, the secret of a long life is: 'Eat less and live longer.' One thing is still strange. The men live longer than the women in Georgia. What is the reason for this difference? The men work less hard than the women and drink more wine ...

How long will *you* live?

Do you want to live to be a hundred? Here are some rules for success. First, choose your parents and grandparents carefully. If they lived to a good old age, so will you. Secondly, live in the right place. If you were not born in

(above) A Hunza woman cooks chapatis.
(left) A peaceful life in the Hunza valley.

Georgia or Ecuador, there are other healthy places in the world, like East Anglia in Britain. Thirdly, choose the right kind of job. Doctors, dentists and bus-drivers die young. Farmers, priests and orchestral conductors live much longer. If you are in the wrong kind of job, you can still improve your way of life. Use the chart on the next page to see how long *you* will live. Then decide what you must change in your life to make it last longer.

How to be a hundred

Plenty of people will give you advice. When he was 80, Dr J. A. Sage wrote a book, *How to be a 100*. In 1975, the 96-year-old doctor was still farming in South Africa. 'I feel better than ever,' he told reporters. 'Old age? I don't believe in it.' Did his ideas work for him? No. Sadly, he died in 1979 at the age of 99. The following advice comes from the successful – people who have lived to be a hundred.

An old man in the Caucasus was talking about his past life. 'I was young then,' he said, as he described his 87th year. His secret and his advice was: 'Think young and stay young.' An old woman from Missouri, USA, gives this advice. 'Drink a little whisky and some warm beer every day.' An English lady centenarian just said, 'Take a cold bath every morning.' On her 102nd birthday Miss Julia Thompson explained the secret of her long and happy life. 'Never have anything to do with men,' she said. The shortest, simplest piece of advice came from Mr Jim Chapman, aged 103. 'Just keep breathing,' he told reporters. What about Mr Izumi? 'I watch TV,' he said, 'and I never worry.'

But do you really want to be a hundred? What's wrong with the old saying, 'Eat, drink and be merry, for tomorrow we die.'?

THIS IS YOUR LIFE

Your basic life expectancy is:-

Year born	Men	Women
1880–1900	35–40	37–42
1901–1910	48	51
1911–1920	51½	56
1921–1930	58½	62
1931–1940	60½	66½
1941–1950	65	70½
1951–1960	67	74
1961–1970	67½	74½

Present Age

1–4	1	56–60	6½
5–20	2	61–65	8
21–25	2½	66–70	9½
26–35	3	71–75	11½
36–40	3½	76–80	12
41–45	4	81–85	6½
46–50	4½	86 plus	4½
51–55	5½		

Add the right figure from the **Present Age** column to your basic life expectancy. Also add one year for every five years your father lived or has lived past the age of 70. Do the same for your mother.

Example: A man born in the year

1931	= 60½
age in 1978	= 4½
father and mother 75	= 2
other scores (net)	= 0

He will probably live until the age of 67

Marital Status: If you are married, add five years. If you are over 25 and not married, deduct one year for every ten years not married.

New Total

...... years

Where you live: If you live in a small town add four years. If you live in a big city, deduct two years.

New Total

...... years

Economic status: If you have been either rich OR poor 'most' of your life, deduct three years.

New Total

...... years

Your shape: If you are over 40, deduct one year for every 2.25kg you are overweight.

New Total

...... years

Exercise: If you take some exercise every day, add three years. If you run, cycle or play tennis every day, add five years.

New Total

...... years

Your character: If you are usually a happy, friendly person, add one to five years. If you often feel angry or frightened, deduct one to five years.

New Total

...... years

Alcohol: If you are a heavy drinker, deduct five years. If you are a very heavy drinker, deduct ten.

New Total

...... years

Smoking: If you smoke 10–20 cigarettes a day, deduct three years; 20–30 deduct five years; more than 30, deduct ten years. But if you smoke a pipe or cigars, deduct two years.

New Total

...... years

General Health: If you see your doctor and dentist twice a year to check your health, add two years. If you are often ill, deduct two years.

FINAL TOTAL

...... years

Notes

polished rice rice without its natural skin.
chapatis a simple kind of bread.

jam made from fruit and a lot of sugar.

Exercises

A Before you read
Study this chart of life expectancy.

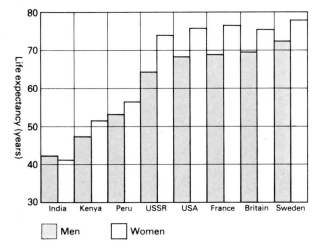

1 Which country has the highest life expectancy and which the lowest?
2 Where do men live longer than women?
3 Can you explain the differences in life expectancy between different countries?

B Read for main points
1 The oldest person in the world lives in:
  (a) Japan (b) S. America (c) the USSR
2 To prove their age old people need:
  (a) death certificates (b) birth certificates (c) medical certificates.
3 Scientists can now work out a person's age from:
  (a) a bone (b) a tooth (c) a hair.
4 The Hunzas live: (a) near the sea (b) on lowland farms (c) in mountain villages.
5 Dr McCarrison was especially interested in:
  (a) work (b) diet (c) exercise.

C Read for detail
1 (a) Find five reasons why very old people may not give their real age.
  (b) Give two reasons why American scientists are waiting for more Russian teeth.
  (c) What three things seem to be very important for a long life?

(d) Work out four ways in which the life of people in Western cities is unhealthy.
(e) Name three jobs which lead to early death.

2 Copy and complete these notes on McCarrison's experiments with rats.

	Group 1	Group 2	Group 3
Diet			white bread, jam, tea
Health			fat, ill
Behaviour			unhappy
Death			Don't know

D Talk about yourself
1 Work out the chart on p. 70. How long will *you* live?
2 Which centenarian's advice do you think is most helpful to you? Why?

E Read for language
1 Find the word for a person who: (a) does experiments (b) tries to stop crime (c) is a religious leader (d) looks after teeth.
2 Write definitions for: (a) a bus-driver (b) a farmer (c) a doctor (d) a lawyer
3 Combine the clauses in A and B to express conditions for a long life.
  A If you eat less,
    If you think young,
    If you eat the right kind of diet,
    If you are in the wrong kind of job,
  B you will have a long, healthy life.
    you will stay young.
    you can still improve your way of life.
    you will live longer.

F News in brief
End of an era
Elsie Hillier, for 45 years village post-mistress at Combe Bay, near Bath, has decided to retire – at the age of 102.

What's her secret?

Amadeo Modigliani 1884–1920
Head of a woman 1918. Oil, 53 × 36cm

Bowl. Greece – early Cycladic.
3200–2700 BC. Marble, height 14cm

Male figure. Mexico – Xochipala
style 1200–900 BC. Clay, 16.3cm

Portrait of Zen priest. Japan – Ashikaga
period 1555. Paint on silk, height 98.6cm

J. Arp *Dream Object* 1941
Bronze, height 24.4cm

WORLD OF ART

Figure of Buddha. Japan – Kamakura period. 13th–14th C. Wood, height 20.6cm

Figure of llama. Peru – Inca style 12th–14th C. Silver, height 23.2cm

Blanket. Alaska c. 1875–90 Goat wool and bark, 187.5cm

Four miles from the ancient city of Norwich is the modern University of East Anglia. Its great grey buildings are set in open, green parkland. One large new building stands out on the west side. It is the Sainsbury Centre for the Visual Arts. In 1973 Sir Robert and Lady Sainsbury decided to give their private art collection to the University. Their son, Mr David Sainsbury, offered to meet the cost of building a home for the collection and of adding new works of art in later years. Sir Robert's grandfather began the family business with one small grocer's shop and there is now a chain of Sainsbury supermarkets. For many years Sir Robert helped his brother run the family business, but in his free time he developed his interest in the world of art. The result is an interesting and valuable collection of paintings and sculpture from many different periods and places.

The University speaks . . .

'This is a wonderful gift. The Sainsburys have built up one of the most beautiful and interesting collections in the modern world. The name of Sainsbury will stand beside those who, from the seventeenth century to the present day, have given British universities their great centres of art. The Ashmolean at Oxford was a gift from Ashmole in 1677. In 1816 Fitzwilliam gave his collection to start the museum of that name in Cambridge. The Courtauld family, in 1932, gave London University its famous Institute and Gallery. Now the name of Sainsbury will live on in the University of East Anglia. This is a very exciting moment in the history of our university. Sir Robert's gift will add greatly to the life of staff and students here. It will give

pleasure to the people of Britain, and, we hope, to visitors from every country in the world. We are all very moved that Sir Robert chose *our* university.'

Sir Robert's story

People often ask Sir Robert, 'When did you start collecting? Why did you decide to become a collector?' His answer is always the same. He never decided to become a collector and he has never thought of himself as a collector in the usual sense of the word. He does not buy works of art to fill a gap in his collection or just because they are rare. If people ask him, 'What are you looking for?' he always replies, 'I am not looking for anything. Works of art find me.' Sir Robert, then, is not a collector. He is just a person who has built up a collection of art. He has been buying works of art for forty years, first as an unmarried man, and then with his wife, Lisa. He buys what he likes. He does not care about the style or the period or fashion in art. If he likes something, if he has room for it, if he has enough money for it, he buys it. His interest in art is personal. He buys with his heart and not with his head.

Sir Robert never studied art, either at school or as a young man, so he has no fixed ideas about what is good or bad. No-one ever told him how he should look at a picture. He discovered art for himself, and he discovered that some works moved him but others did not. If other people admired a work of art but he did not like it, then he would not buy it. Sir Robert tells a story about a visit to an art gallery in Paris. The owner showed him a primitive African statue, and named the price. Sir Robert turned away.

'Aren't you going to buy it?' asked the owner.

'No,' said Sir Robert.

'Why not? You agree it's genuine?'

'Yes, as far as I know.'

'You agree it's rare.'

'Oh yes, without a doubt.'

'You agree it's a fair price.'

'Yes.'

'Then why don't you buy it?'

'Because I don't want it.'

The gallery owner could not believe it. Sir Robert must be mad. What more could a collector want? The statue was a genuine piece, rare, and a fair price. But Sir Robert did not buy it, and he never went back to that gallery.

With sculpture he discovered the joys of touching and holding a work of art. He particularly likes very small objects and there

The University and the Centre from the air.

are many in his gift to the university. His journey through the world of art has been full of the joys of discovery. He has found new art forms that move him as much as the old and famous. So, in buying works of art, he just chooses what he likes. As he explains:

'I know that art scholars see more in a work of art than I can, but I enjoy art as much as they do. You can learn things about art, but no-one can teach you to enjoy it. That comes from inside you. I was born with the ability to love art. Do not misunderstand me. I admire scholars and use their knowledge to help me. But in my life as a businessman I've never had time to study art properly. I have learnt a lot from my friends in the art world, from experience, from using my eyes and hands.'

Sir Robert has not travelled through the world of art alone. He started buying paintings as a young, unmarried man but since his marriage his wife has travelled with him, and they have shared the joys and the discovery. Together they have made their discoveries and together they have found great happiness in art. So why are they giving their collection away? Many people have asked Sir Robert, 'Why a university? Why a new university? Why the University of East Anglia? And why have a Centre for Visual Arts? Why not just build a museum or art gallery?' These are Sir Robert and Lady Sainsbury's reasons:

'We wanted to give young men and women the chance to work near art, and the chance to live with art. A new university is the best place for a new way of looking at art.'

The architect speaks . . .

'At our first meeting Sir Robert and Lady Sainsbury explained their ideas about art galleries. They did not want their collection in a museum but in a building which would allow people to enjoy works of art as part of their daily life. In a university they wanted scientists as well as arts students to enjoy the collection, and to share the experience of art. So one of our first decisions was to make the gallery a meeting place for people. We chose a site in the valley which could be joined to the main university buildings by a bridge. The

75

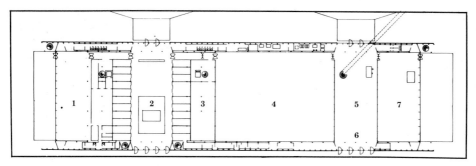

1 Restaurant
2 School of Fine Arts and Music (Art History Sector)
3 Study area
4 Living area/display gallery
5 Conservatory
6 Coffee bar
7 Special exhibition area

Plan of the Sainsbury Centre.

nearest were the science laboratories, so we have really brought the sciences and arts together. The place we chose also had beautiful views to the south and west.

'Next we visited different art galleries in Europe and the United States to get ideas for the building itself. We decided these were the most important points:

1 Good natural light from above.
2 Room for the gallery to change and grow.
3 Plenty of storage space.
4 Good security – we needed to protect the collection without having security men everywhere.
5 Easy ways of making changes or doing repairs. We did not want to close the gallery or move the exhibits to repair one light!
6 A design which brought everything together – furniture and display, and people with different interests.

We discussed our ideas with the University and they developed. We decided to include the School of Fine Art, the Senior Common Room and a new restaurant for the university and the public in the Centre. And outside we decided to build a 16-hectare lake.

'We looked at many different forms of building. Our final design grouped all the activities under one roof, so the building is in the shape of a long tube.

'Teaching is close to viewing, and people pass through the display galleries, both students and staff, on their way to lectures or to lunch. The building is 7.5m high, 35m wide and 131.4m long. The end walls are made of glass, so people can sit and enjoy the view of the new lake at one end or the trees at the other. People can enter the gallery from the bridge and come down the stairs, or through the front door at ground level. Here there is an entrance conservatory – with reception, security, a coffee bar and a general meeting place. To one side there is a special exhibition room. To the other is the main 'living area'. This seemed the best word for a space with easy chairs, low tables and art books, all surrounded by the works of the Sainsbury collection. The works of art themselves are hung on screens or placed on stands. This means we can move or change exhibits easily. Underground, in the basement, there are workshops and storage space.

'The building tries to match the collection, to go beyond fashion, style, particular artists and periods. The collector, the architect, the University, we all worked together. The first designer was Kho Lang Le, a Dutch Indonesian. He died during the early stages of the work, but his ideas live on in the Centre. It is a living home for one man's world of art.'

Notes
Fine Arts painting and sculpture.
arts subjects all non-science subjects: literature, languages, etc.

Senior Common Room a meeting place for the teachers in a university.
conservatory a room with glass walls for growing indoor plants.

Exercises

A Before you read
1 Study the works of art on p. 72 and 73.
Which do you think is (a) most beautiful
(b) most interesting (c) most valuable?
2 If you had enough money to be an art collector,
what would you buy and why?

B Read for ideas
1 Which of these reasons for buying works of art
are true for Sir Robert Sainsbury?
   (a) it is rare
   (b) it is beautiful
   (c) he wants to fill a gap in his collection
   (d) he likes it
   (e) it is in fashion
   (f) it is in a certain style
   (g) it moves him
   (h) it is famous
   (i) he has enough money for it
   (j) it's a fair price
   (k) he has enough room for it
2 In what ways is the Sainsbury Centre different
from a traditional art gallery?
3 Where did the architect look for ideas and who
did he discuss them with?
4 What were the good points of the site chosen?

C Read for detail
1 Copy and complete this table.

Date	Museum/ Gallery	University	City
. . . . .	The Ashmolean	. . . .	Oxford
. . . . .	The Fitzwilliam Museum	. . . .	. . . .
. . . . .	The Courtauld Institute	London	. . . .
. . . . .	. . . .	East Anglia	. . . .

2 Classify the exhibits on p. 72 and 73. Which
ones come from:
(a) North America (b) South America
(c) Europe (d) the Far East?
3 (a) Which piece of sculpture is the smallest?
   (b) Which exhibit is the most modern?
   (c) Which is the oldest work of art?
4 What are people doing in the picture on
p. 74/75? List the activities you can see.

D What's your opinion?
1 What do you think of the the architecture of the
Sainsbury Centre?
2 Which is your favourite museum or art gallery?
Describe it.

E Read for language
1 Give the name and number on the plan of the
part of the centre where people go: (a) for a meal
(b) for a coffee (c) to see the main collection
(d) to view special exhibits (e) to study.
2 The artists used oil on canvas, ink on silk, wool
and bark for the paintings and hangings on p. 72
and 73. Make a list of the materials used for the
sculptures.
3 Write a dialogue between a reporter and Sir
Robert Sainsbury. Ask:
   –when he started collecting
   –why he decided to become a collector
   –what he's looking for now
   –how he chooses works of art
   –what kind of sculpture he likes
   –how he learned about art
   –if his wife shares his love of art
   –why they are giving their collection to a new
   university
Find suitable answers from the text on p. 74 and
75.

F Make a collection
Find a picture or postcard of your favourite work of
art. Bring it to class to show other students. Make a
display of all the pictures.

13 How to win the Sales War

The Sales War happens twice a year, every January and July. People go to the Sales to save money. Shops have Sales to make money. And they do. A big department store can take £1,000,000 of their customers' money in one day. And too many customers go home with ugly, useless purchases. 'If you make anything cheap enough,' says Paul Walker, manager of a large store in London, 'someone will buy it.' We all have sales mistakes in our cupboards. My friend Julia once bought a cashmere sweater in a sale. It's one size too small – it's a 12 and she takes a 14. The colour – a strange green – makes her look ill. 'But it's cashmere,' she cries. 'The price was reduced from £50 to £30 in the sale. So I saved £20.' But she didn't. She wasted £30 because she never wears the sweater. A real bargain is not just cheap. It is something you really need and often use. If you want to get real bargains in the January and July Sales, learn the rules of the Sales War and keep them. Don't let the stores always win.

Understand the system

The stores have two main seasons, winter and summer. Sometimes the buyers make mistakes. They order too many goods and the shop cannot sell them all. Or they choose a bad colour or a poor design. If no-one likes the goods, no-one buys them. In a wet summer the shops can't sell summer dresses or bikinis – and customers can't buy raincoats. They are for the winter season. A train strike in winter means people cannot get to the shops in the big cities. Then it's time for the new season, but the stores are still full of old stock. They have no money to buy new goods from the manufacturers, and no room for them in the store. So, twice a year, they try to sell all their old stock, fast. They put their prices down and advertise – in the newspapers, on the radio

First in the queue – a couple sleep outside a store.

and on TV. 'Come to the Sales' 'Great Bargains' 'Everything must go.'

The careful, beautiful window displays disappear. Instead the windows are packed with goods and large notices saying SALE SALE SALE. Inside the store everything changes too. 'We want the store to look like a market,' says the manager. 'There must be lots of goods in big piles. We want the customer to feel free. Free to look, free to touch, free to spend.' And spend . . .

There are extra sales assistants to take your money, and extra security staff to catch the thieves. 'Thieves are always a problem,' a security man explains, 'but it's worse during the Sales. It's difficult to see them in the crowds. And ordinary people do strange things in Sales. A lot of them put things in their bags and "forget" to pay . . .' All the staff have extra training before the Sales, and they all do extra work. They are ready for the First Day. Are the customers?

Learn the language of the Sales

There are three main kinds of goods in a sale. First, there are the things the store has not sold that season. These goods have been on sale in the store for at least a month at the normal price. For the sales their price is reduced. Look for this kind of price-tag.

You can find good bargains, but always ask yourself, 'Why has no one wanted to buy this before?'

Then there are 'Special Offers', 'Special Purchases' or just 'Specials'. These goods come straight from the manufacturers. They too have to clear their stock at the end of each season, so they sell their goods to the stores at a lower price. The stores put these extra goods into the sales. But ask yourself, 'Why couldn't the manufacturer sell them to the stores for the normal price?'

Manufacturers also sell 'seconds' to the stores for the sales. Second-class goods, or 'seconds' have something wrong with them, but the ordinary customer cannot usually see it. Perhaps one line isn't straight, or the colours are not quite right. A second from the manufacturer is usually a very good bargain. Here the rule is: 'If you need it and like it, buy it.' Also look for the words 'shop-soiled' or 'damaged'. Shops can't sell a dirty dress for the full price, but you can take it home and wash it. If one leg on a table is loose the shop has to reduce the price, but it may only take ten minutes to repair. Ask yourself, 'How long does anything stay perfect in my house?' If you see a good bargain, seize it.

Follow the rules for the Sales shopper

Before the Sales start

1 Know what you want and look for it. Look in all the shop windows and go round the stores before the Sales start. Decide what you need and can afford. And remember where it is.

2 Find the quickest way to each department. This will save time on the day.

On the day

1 Wear comfortable clothes. Do wear flat shoes, and don't wear a thick coat – it will be very hot. If you want to buy clothes, wear a skirt not trousers. It will save time in the changing rooms.

2 Leave your family and friends at home. If you must go to the Sales with other people, agree to shop separately. Fix a time and place for a meeting later in the day, and keep to it. It's very easy to lose people in the Sales.

3 Don't drink too much tea or coffee. If you do, you will spend all day in the queue for the toilets, not the queue for the bargains.

4 Arrive early. The best things in a sale always go in the first half-hour. And they go to the people from the front of the queue.

5 Go straight to your bargain. Buy it and get out. Do not stop. Do not look around you. Do not buy anything else. Remember, the store wants your money and has many ways of getting it. Keep to the golden rule: 'Know what you want, and only buy what you need.'

'I was a salesgirl in the Sales'

Students never have enough money, so they try to find jobs in the holidays. Economics student Sue Smith was a salesgirl in the Sales. Here she tells her story from the shop assistant's side of the counter.

'I got a month's work from a famous store in the January Sales. We started work at the end of December – three days' special training ready for the First Day of the Sales. On the evening of the great day itself we got our final orders. "Take your shoes off," they told us. (It's a very good store and has thick carpets) "You'll move more quickly without shoes and you will be more comfortable." They told the ladies, "Wear trousers, not dresses or skirts." That was very strange. (It is a very old store and the lady assistants never wear anything as modern as trousers.) Finally they told us, "Stay behind the counter. Do not come out from behind your counter. Always keep the counter between you and the customers." Was this to hide our trousers and feet? "Oh no," laughed one of the regular assistants. "It's for our safety. The customers could kill you." (In *that* store? The customers are people of good family, the shop assistants always polite and helpful . . .)

'With these three simple but strange rules in my ears I went home for a good night's sleep. The next morning, after a large breakfast, I left for work. At 8.55 I was ready, in my trousers and cotton socks, behind my counter. They had put me in the Dress Fabrics Department on the ground floor. Through the windows I could see hundreds of women. They were all wearing flat shoes and holding very large bags. And they did look rather dangerous. At nine o'clock our strong, silent security men went slowly to the doors and unlocked them. They then ran – yes, ran – back into the store. I had seen security men run after people before, but *away* from them . . .? What were they afraid of? I soon found out.

'The women outside poured through the doors like a hungry army. They were rushing straight at my counter. "Why aren't I in a safer place," I thought, "like Grand Pianos on the fourth floor?" But they didn't attack me, and they didn't stop. They ran on, pushing each other and knocking over piles of dress fabric. They disappeared into other departments, into the lifts, up the stairs, down into the basement. "They'll be back," said the regular assistants. "They always go to China and Glass first, then Radio and TV." Half an hour later they appeared again, pushing, shouting, seizing materials, arguing about the price. All day I cut cloth, packed it and took their money. And I lived to tell the tale. I learned more about economics in that one month than in three years at university.'

Tales from the Sales

£10 LETTER. WE ASKED: What's happened to you at the Sales? £10 goes to the sender of the first letter and £2 to each of the others.

Body for sale

We needed a new shed for the garden and we saw one in a big store – reduced from £40 to £25.

On the first day of the Sales I was the first customer in the shop. I rushed to the gardening department, and up to the shed. I opened the door, then screamed. There was a body on the floor. My screams brought people from all over the store. They also woke up the 'body'. 'I hid in the shed last night,' the man explained. 'I wanted to be first in the shop this morning.'

MRS D. GREENALL
Heaton Chapel, Cheshire.

Sales Talk

I saw a bargain blouse in a Sale and went along at 6.0 a.m. to queue. There were two women in front of me, so I asked if they wanted the blouse. They said they didn't, and started to talk to each other. They had both been in hospital and were describing their illnesses and operations in great detail. Their talk made *me* feel ill. So I had to go home – without the blouse.

M. WILLIAMS
Ramsgate, Kent.

False Alarm

I was trying on a dress in the Sales. Suddenly the store's alarm bell went off. 'It's a bomb,' someone shouted. I ran into the street in my bra and skirt. The other shoppers all laughed at me, but a kind policeman gave me his coat. The crowd cheered. The bomb? It was a false alarm.

MRS B. PETERS
Port St. Mary, Isle of Wight

Sales Service

I queued for several hours to buy a beautiful new bed at a bargain price. I was the first person inside the store, so I got first-class service. The manager took me up to the furniture department himself.

But when we arrived my bargain bed had gone. The person behind me in the queue had hurried past us and bought it! I have never queued for a bargain again. I've learned my lesson!

MRS C. LLEWELLYN
Stockwood, Avon

One month before my baby was born I went to the Sales. I'd seen a sewing machine for just £15.00. I waited for two hours in the queue. At last it started to move, and so did I. I fell down in a faint. When I opened my eyes again I was inside the store. One of the staff was looking after me. 'What about my sewing machine?' I asked weakly. 'I'm afraid they've all gone,' he said, 'but I'll get you another one, at the sale price, I promise. It'll arrive before the baby.' And it did, two weeks later. Now, when I'm making clothes on my bargain sewing machine, I always remember that kind assistant.

MRS J. CRAWFORD
Langley, Hants.

Notes
department store a large shop with different departments on each floor.

Exercises

A Before you read

1 Study the advertisement on p. 79. Which clothes would you buy? How much could you save?
2 Look quickly through the whole unit and put this list of text types in order:
(a) explanation of word meanings (b) a list of instructions (c) letters to a newspaper (d) a statement of the topic (e) a personal narrative (f) a description of a system
3 Why do people go to the Sales? Why do shops have Sales? Make a list of reasons. Compare your list with (a) other people's ideas, (b) the information on p. 78 and 79.

B Read for ideas

1 When are the Sales held?
2 What is a real bargain?
3 Why are stores full of old stock at the end of the season? Find three reasons.
4 Is there any new stock in the Sales?
5 How do customers know there's Sale on?
6 What's different about the stores in the Sales?
7 What kinds of extra staff are needed? Why?
8 Was Sue Smith a regular or an extra sales assistant?
9 What surprised her about (a) the instructions to staff (b) the behaviour of the security staff (c) the customers?
10 Which letter do you find funniest? Why?

C Read for detail

1 Find the right words for:
(a) It was on sale at a higher price.
(b) The manufacturer has sold it to the store for a lower price.
(c) It has got dirty in the shop.
(d) Part of it is broken.

2 Read this tale from the Sales. Look at the Rules on p. 80. Which rules were broken?

'Mrs Smith decided to go to the Sales with her friend Mrs Jones and buy a bargain cashmere sweater. They arrived in London at 10.30 and stopped at a cafe for a drink. Then they found the right store. On the way to the Knitwear Department Mrs Jones saw some cheap evening dresses. 'Oh, I must try that blue one on,' she cried. Mrs Smith, in her thick winter coat, began to feel hot and uncomfortable in the changing room, so she went to the Cloakroom. There was a long queue and when she returned to Evening Wear Mrs Jones had disappeared. 'Perhaps she is waiting for me in Knitwear,' thought Mrs Smith. But Mrs Jones was not there, and there were no cashmere sweaters left either. So Mrs Smith bought a fairisle sweater instead. When she got home, she found it was too small.'

D Talk about the Sales

1 Can you tell a tale from the Sales?
2 Describe your best and worst purchases ever.
3 Would you like a job as a shop assistant?

E Read for language

1 In which department of a big store will you find:
(a) a sweater (b) a shirt (c) a shed (d) a bed (e) trousers (f) a tea-set (g) cassettes

2 Rephrase the instructions to extra staff (see p. 81) using *must* or *must not*.
Example: You *must* take your shoes off.

F Be prepared!

Make a list of sizes for members of your family from this international chart.

Women's Clothes Sizes	Britain	8	10	12	14	16	18	20
	USA	6	8	10	12	14	16	18
	Europe	36	38	40	42	44	46	48
Men's Shirt Sizes	Britain	14	$14\frac{1}{2}$	15	$15\frac{1}{2}$	16	$16\frac{1}{2}$	17
	USA (ins)							
	Europe (cms)	36	$37\frac{1}{2}$	38	39	40	41	42

14 THE GUITAR

the most popular instrument in the world

The people of the world speak many different languages, but everyone understands one special language – music. In Africa or Australia, South America or Scandinavia, people sing or play musical instruments. There are many kinds of musical instrument but one is famous all over the world – the guitar. Everyone can understand the music of the guitar, and nearly everyone likes its sound. Guitar music is a world language, and the guitar is the most popular instrument in the world.

The instrument. Meet the guitar family

The guitar has a long history. In Ancient Egypt people played simple stringed instruments like this:

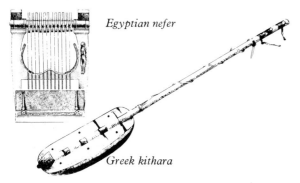

Egyptian nefer

Greek kithara

The Greeks and the Romans also made music by plucking strings with their fingers, and the word 'guitar' comes from the Latin 'cithara'.

The first true guitars appeared during the fifteenth century in Spain. At first it was an instrument for poor people and travelling musicians, but soon rich people all over Europe were learning to play the guitar.

The guitar travelled fast and far. When Cortés landed in Mexico in 1519, he had a guitar player with his soldiers. A century later an English visitor to Mexico heard American Indians playing the Spanish guitar. Then, in 1650, a Spanish soldier wrote in a letter from Argentina, 'I went to a wedding and we sang to the guitar.' The Spanish Americans made some changes to the instrument and developed their own style of playing. In Spain itself, the flamenco guitar became as popular as the classical guitar. Then in North America new kinds of music, folk and jazz especially, led to new kinds of guitar. So, the early Spanish guitar has become the father of a family of instruments.

In the modern world there are four main kinds of guitar: the classical, the flamenco, the steel-stringed and the electric guitar. Today members of the guitar family are everywhere – in cafés, at parties, in concert halls and at pop festivals. At any hour of the day or night one thing is certain. Someone somewhere is playing the guitar.

Watteau: *Gilles and his family.*

The players: master and pupil

The greatest classical guitarist this century, Andrés Segovia, was born in the south of Spain in 1893. He started to learn the piano, but decided to change to the guitar. When he could not find a teacher in his home town of Jaen he had to learn to play by himself. At the age of fourteen he gave his first public concert in Granada. He also gave recitals in Cordoba and Seville, and then went to Madrid. He was an immediate success in the capital city, and soon received many invitations to perform abroad. In 1925 he played in the Soviet Union, and three years later he gave the first ever guitar recital in New York. No one ever forgets a concert by Segovia.

'He is a master of the guitar. Every note is magic. People come in thousands to hear him play, but you always feel that he is playing for you alone.'

Segovia is more than a great performer. He has discovered wonderful old music for the guitar and arranged music written for other instruments. Many modern composers have written new pieces especially for Segovia, including Manuel de Falla and Villa-Lobos. And Segovia is a great teacher too. Many famous players have studied with him.

One of Segovia's pupils, John Williams, was born in Australia in 1941. At the age of eleven he came to Britain with his family, and his father took him to play to Segovia. He immediately agreed to teach the boy at his summer school in Siena, and advised him to continue his studies at the Academy there. After five years in Italy John Williams returned to England, and in 1958 gave his first public recital at London's Wigmore Hall. In the words of Segovia himself, 'A prince of the guitar has arrived in the musical world. It will not be long before his name is famous in England and abroad.'

Segovia – master of the guitar.

Segovia was right, and John Williams is now a world-famous classical guitarist. But he is not only interested in the classical guitar and its music. He has also learned to play the electric guitar and includes works of many different styles in his concerts. In 1979 he formed his own pop group, *Sky*, with four other musicians. *Sky* has been a great success on radio, on records, on TV and in live performance. As John Williams himself says:

'The guitar has always been a popular instrument. We must never forget that. Popular music is different from classical music, but it's just as good.'

John Williams with his pop group Sky.

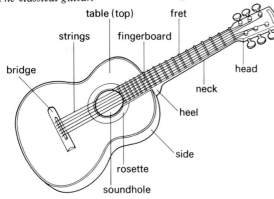

The classical guitar.

table (top) fret
strings fingerboard
bridge head
neck
heel
side
rosette
soundhole

The Makers: Spanish guitars from an English village

Factories can produce thousands of cheap guitars, but the best modern instruments are still made the old way – by hand in small workshops. One famous maker of classical guitars is José Romanillos. He lives and works in the English village of Semley. Here he talks to Tom Evans about making guitars.

Shaping the sides with a hot iron.

Evans: How did you become a guitar-maker?

Romanillos: I wanted to play the guitar, but I didn't have enough money to buy one. So, I bought some wood and made my first guitar – on a kitchen table in London.

Evans: How long ago was that?

Romanillos: 1959. Over twenty years ago, and I haven't stopped since then.

Evans: How many guitars do you make in a year?

Romanillos: From fourteen to seventeen. That's all. I work alone, and I do almost everything by hand. It's slow, but it gives the best results.

Evans: What are your instruments like?

Romanillos: I try to make guitars that both look and sound good. I prefer small guitars, with a clear, strong sound. I'm always searching for ways to get a better sound. I always hope the next instrument will be special. The most important thing is the wood. You need very good wood for good guitars.

Evans: What wood do you use?

Romanillos: I use different kinds of wood for different parts of the guitar. I buy spruce, a pale softwood from the Swiss Alps, for the top or 'table'. I go and choose the tree myself. For the back and sides I use rosewood – a dark hardwood from India or Brazil. Then I use Honduras cedar, a red wood, for the neck, and black ebony for the fingerboard.

Evans: How do you start making a guitar?

Romanillos: Well, I work on four guitars at once. First I make the sides. The wood is cut into pieces 0.6 cm thick at the mill. Then I plane the pieces by hand until I get just the right thickness. I use a hot iron to shape the sides.

Evans: Is that difficult?

Romanillos: Yes. You need a lot of practice before you can get the right shape. Next I cut the different

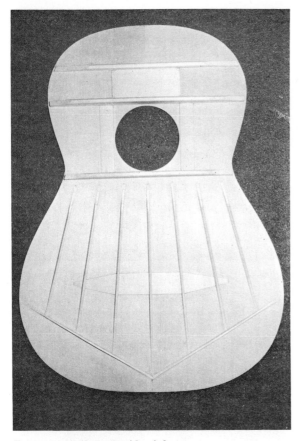

Fan struts on the underside of the top.

Tapping the 'table' to test the sound.

parts of the neck and the heel. I leave the neck a rough shape, but finish the inside part of the heel. I make the grooves ready for the sides of the guitar.

Evans: What about the top?

Romanillos: That's made from two halves of spruce. I join them together and glue them. Then I plane the wood to the right thickness and put in the rosette.

Evans: Does the rosette change the sound?

Romanillos: No, not at all. It just looks beautiful. Every maker chooses his own design. Mine comes from the wonderful arches in the mosque of Cordoba. For a good sound you must get the top the right thickness, and the struts too. The struts are thin pieces of spruce that go on the underside of the top. I usually follow Torres' pattern of seven struts in the shape of a fan. I test the sound again and again. I hold the top to my ear and tap it. After a time, you get a 'feel' for the right sound.

Evans: How do you make the back?

Romanillos: I use a piece of rosewood in two halves. I work on the back and the front at the same time. They must match each other. When I've finished the top and back, I'm ready to glue the parts together. First I glue the sides into the neck, and then fix the top to the sides. Finally I glue the back onto the sides and wait for it to dry.

Evans: That finishes the body then?

Romanillos: Yes, almost. But there's a lot of

	other work to do. I must be sure the neck is at the right angle. Then I have to make the head, and shape and fix the fingerboard.
Evans:	How do you fit the frets onto the fingerboard?
Romanillos:	I have a piece of wood with the positions of the frets marked – 65 cm apart. Then I cut grooves into the fingerboard with a special saw. It cuts the right depth and width. The frets are made from nickel silver wire, 2 mm thick, and I just tap it gently into the grooves.
Evans:	Is the guitar ready for the strings yet?
Romanillos:	No, not quite. I have to shape the neck properly and fix the bridge. I use a very strong modern glue to fix the bridge onto the top. When the glue is dry I put on the strings and try out every note. Sometimes I change the top a little, but not often.
Evans:	When do you put the varnish on?
Romanillos:	Well, I hang new guitars up in the workshop for a few weeks. I try them out and get to know them. Then finally I varnish them. That's a long, slow job, but you can't make a guitar in a hurry. And you can't learn to make guitars quickly. Stradivarius made his first violin when he was eleven, and his best ones after he was fifty! I'm still learning.

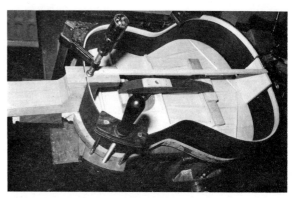

Gluing the sides to the neck and top.

Cutting grooves in the fingerboard for the frets.

Tapping the frets into the grooves.

Exercises

A Before you read
1 Which kind of music do you prefer: classical, jazz, folk, pop? When and where do you listen to music?
2 The text is in three parts after a short introduction. Look quickly through the text and decide which part is: (a) an illustrated interview (b) a biography (c) a short history

B Read for ideas
1 Complete these sentences:
(a) In ancient . . . people played simple stringed . . . .
(b) The first true guitars came from . . . and were played by . . . people.
(c) Then rich people in . . . started to learn to . . . the guitar.
(d) . . . soldiers took . . . with them to America.
(e) New kinds of . . . and instruments developed in Spain and . . . .
(f) So, in the . . . world there is a . . . of guitars.

2 Compare text and pictures:
(a) Which pictures illustrate the ideas in sentences (a) and (c) above?
(b) In which picture does the guitar match the diagram on p. 86?
(c) What are the differences between Segovia and John Williams? Compare age, musical education, career, special interests, etc.

3 Check the facts:
(a) Why did Romanillos make his first guitar?
(b) Why doesn't he make hundreds of guitars a year?
(c) What is most important for a good sound?
(d) Can you learn to make guitars quickly?

C What do you think?
1 How is music different from other languages?
2 Can everyone in the world understand it?
3 Is popular music as good as classical music?

D Read for detail
1 Find, or work out, the date of:
(a) Cortes' landing in Mexico.
(b) Segovia's first public concert.
(c) The first guitar recital in New York.
(d) John Williams' first arrival in Britain.
(e) Romanillos' first guitar.

2 This is the *Who's Who* entry for John Williams.

> **WILLIAMS, John,** OBE 1980; guitarist; *b* Melbourne, 24 April 1941. Studied with father, Segovia and at the Accademia Musicale Chigiana, Siena and RCM, London; since when has given many recitals and concerts, and made recordings of both solo guitar, and chamber and orchestral music. Mem., Sky, 1979-. *Recreations:* people, living, chess, table-tennis, music. *Address: c/o* Harold Holt Ltd, 31 Sinclair Road, W14.

(a) Underline any information which is NOT in the text on p. 85.
(b) Write a *Who's Who* entry for Segovia.

E Read for language
1 Complete this table from the text on p. 86.

Wood	Country	Part of guitar
Spruce Rosewood Cedar Ebony	Switzerland Brazil, ... Honduras Sri Lanka	. . . . . back and . . . .

2 Choose the right word for each definition:
(a) *varnish/glue:* it gives wood a clear, hard bright finish.
(b) *factory/workshop:* a building where many things are made by machines.
(c) *saw/plane:* a large knife with many teeth used to cut wood.

3 Describe how Romanillos makes a guitar. Begin: *First he chooses the wood.*

F Tailpiece
'We don't like their sound. Groups of guitars are on the way out.'
Who said it? When? Which group were they talking about?
(*Answer: see p. 96.*)

15 THE PLEASURES OF PICNICS

Picnics past and present

Some people have always had to eat away from home – farmworkers in the fields, hunters in the forests, and travellers on the road. Others choose to eat in the open air. They take their lunch or tea out into the countryside and have a picnic. It's a strange word – 'picnic'. It may come from an old French word, 'pique-nique', and it was once spelled 'Pick Nick'. In English it used to mean a meal to which each guest brought a different dish.

'A picnic supper,' says *The Times* of March 18, 1802, 'consists of many different dishes. Before the night each guest receives a menu with a number against one dish. Then he has to provide the dish marked with his number. He can take it with him in his carriage or send it by a servant.'

These picnic suppers were more like a grand dinner party than a country picnic. They were usually held indoors in rich dining rooms, but sometimes tables were laid outside in the gardens of stately homes. Soon 'picnic' came to mean any outdoor party with food. In the summer months both rich and poor people went out into the woods and fields for May Day and Midsummer picnics. When workers moved from the country to new jobs in the towns they returned at weekends for picnics – food tastes better in the fresh air. And they needed a rest from the noise and dirt of the cities. Today picnics are as popular as ever: ordinary family picnics or splendid outdoor parties.

A picnic at Netley Abbey, Hampshire, in 1883.

Claude Monet. Sketch for *Picnic*, 1865–66. Oil on canvas, 1.8 × 1.2m. Pushkin Museum, Moscow.

Portrait of a picnic

The French call a picnic 'a meal on the grass' and one of the world's most beautiful paintings is a portrait of a French picnic. It shows a group of middle-class people at a picnic in the forests of Fontainebleu near Paris. The artist was the great impressionist painter, Claude Monet, who lived from 1840 to 1926. Monet loved good food, his friends and the fresh air of the forests outside Paris. He wrote to a friend, 'I wanted to get out of Paris and try to paint a real picture of a real picnic. The figures were life-size. They were real people. I wanted the painting to be just as real as a photo, my own modern idea of a picnic out of

doors. I lived in a world of sunlight and shadows. It was pure magic.' Monet started work in 1865, but sadly he never finished his life-size painting. He could not pay the rent on his large studio and he had to move to a small room. All that the world has now is an oil sketch for the final work, and two pieces from the final canvas. The marvellous oil sketch in Moscow, full of light and joy, gives an idea of Monet's great plan for a painting 4.5 × 6 m. The two pieces show the beauty of the parts he finished.

The models for the people in the painting were his wife, Camille, and his great friend

Claude Monet. *Picnic* (detail). Oil on canvas. Louvre, Paris.

and fellow artist, Bazille. We can see them, in their fine nineteenth-century fashions, in the left-hand piece now in the Louvre. In the Moscow sketch we can see the whole party. One man has taken off his jacket and is half-lying on the grass. Another leans against a tree, a glass of wine in his hand. The sunlight shines through the trees onto the women in their pretty summer dresses. The centre of the painting shows us the picnic cloth on the grass, with plates and glasses for everyone. And we can see the food, a pâté in pastry, a roast chicken, apples, pears and grapes, bottles of wine and loaves of bread. We can even see a Cupid's heart and arrow with the initial P on the tree to the right. Monet has captured the spirit of a summer picnic and has given us a portrait of real people who now live for ever. Here are the young men and women of nineteenth-century Paris who liked to escape from their weekday jobs and the busy city into the peace of the forest at weekends – for a picnic.

A very English picnic

Gwen Raverat, granddaughter of Charles Darwin, describes a Cambridge picnic early in the twentieth century.

'One day we ourselves arranged a picnic. No-one could call it a success. It was just before Frances' wedding. Her father, my uncle Frank, did not want to lose his daughter,

92

At the picnic. Left to right: Uncle Frank, Uncle Horace, Aunt Etty, Aunt Ida, my mother. My father has already left. He couldn't face all the miseries, and has started off alone to walk home. Aunt Ida alone still has a brave smile on her face. The others are just waiting miserably for the end of the afternoon.

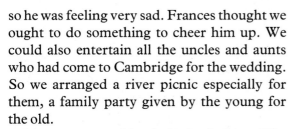

so he was feeling very sad. Frances thought we ought to do something to cheer him up. We could also entertain all the uncles and aunts who had come to Cambridge for the wedding. So we arranged a river picnic especially for them, a family party given by the young for the old.

It was a grey, cold, windy day in June. The aunts wore fur coats and sat close together in the boats. They had to hold onto their heavy hats in the strong wind. The uncles, wrapped in winter coats and thick woollen scarves, were miserably uncomfortable on the hard, narrow seats. And they clearly thought they would die from the cold. But it was even worse when they had to sit down to have tea on the wet grass. There were so many miseries, which we young ones had never noticed at all: nettles, insects and cow-pats, besides the biting wind. Cook had put the tea in bottles – there were no thermos flasks then – and wrapped warm cloths round them. We didn't discover that she had made a terrible mistake until we opened the bottles and poured out the tea. She had put sugar in all the tea. It was the worst moment of the afternoon. No-one could speak. The aunts and uncles all hated sugar in their tea. Besides, it was Immoral. At last Uncle Frank said, in his most bitter voice, "I can forgive the sugar, but I can't forgive the mistake." This was half a joke, but at his words we lost all hope in our picnic and almost in life itself. "Everything goes wrong in this world," we thought sadly. It was too late to save the picnic, so, as quickly as possible, we took the aunts and uncles home to a good fire.'

93

The Teddy Bears' Picnic

In 1979 there was a very special picnic at Longleat in Wiltshire, stately home of the Marquess of Bath. It was for all the people who love Teddy Bears and, of course, for their bears. They came from all over the world, big bears and little bears, bald old bears, and furry young ones. There were Rupert Bears, Paddington Bears, Pooh Bears and Yogi Bears.

All of them were fat, and they were very hungry. People brought marmalade sandwiches for Paddington Bear, honey-cakes for Yogi Bear and whole pots of honey for Pooh Bear. When all the bears had had enough to eat everyone sang the famous picnic song: 'The Teddy Bears' Picnic'.

These Teddy Bears are the Barratt Freefall Team, with the Marquis of Bath and Lord Christopher Thynne at Longleat House.

94

Exercises

A Before you read

1 Look at the people in the pictures on pages 90–93. Who are they? What are they all doing? Do they look happy or sad? Why?

2 The text is in four parts, an introduction and three examples. Match the topic of each part to its title.

Portrait of a picnic	Report of an event
A very English picnic	Discussion of a work of art
The Teddy Bears' Picnic	A short history of picnics
Picnics past and present	A personal account of a picnic

B Read for ideas

1 What kind of people have to eat out of doors?
2 Were the first picnics outdoors?
3 Why do people choose to eat out of doors?
4 Why did Monet decide to paint such a large picture?
5 Who are the people in the portrait?
6 Why didn't Monet finish the painting?
7 Who arranged the family picnic and why?
8 Which was the worst problem?
  (a) They had to sit on wet grass.
  (b) There was a strong, cold wind.
  (c) There were nettles and insects.
  (d) There was sugar in their tea.
  (e) The boat was uncomfortable.
9 How did the Teddy Bears' Picnic end?

C Read for detail

Choose the correct answer

1 Claude Monet was born in (a) 1840 (b) 1865 (c) 1926
2 The Pushkin Museum is in (a) London (b) Paris (c) Moscow
3 Frances was Gwen Raverat's (a) sister (b) cousin (c) aunt
4 Longleat is (a) a stately home (b) an abbey (c) a forest

D Talk about picnics

1 When did you last have a meal out of doors? Where, why and with whom?
2 What did you eat and drink?
3 Were there any problems?

E Read for language

1 Complete this chart.

	Food	Drink	Equipment
Netley			
Monet	bread	wine	plates
Raverat			basket
Longleat	honey		
Modern			

2 Look carefully at the three people in both Monet paintings. Say in which picture
  (a) the man on the left has a beard.
  (b) the woman in the middle is wearing a red and green dress.
  (c) the woman in the middle is wearing a large hat.
  Can you find any other differences?

3 Write a description of the modern picnic on p. 92–93. Describe the people, their clothes, the weather, the setting, the food. Use these phrases: *on the left   on the right   in the centre we can see   the photo shows us*

F Quiz

1 What do you know about famous bears?
  (a) Which bear is named after a London station?
  (b) Which bear comes from the USA?
  (c) Which bear appears in British comics?
  (d) Which bear belonged to a boy called Christopher Robin?
2 What do these symbols mean?
  1.   2.   3.

(Answers: see p. 96)

Answers

Acknowledgements

The author would like to thank the following individuals
and organisations for their help in the preparation of this
book: Linda Townsend, Robert Spencer, William and Joan
Vincent, Charles and Anne Foster, The London Cycling
Campaign, The Sports Council, World Wildlife Fund, Royal
National Institute for the Deaf.

We should like to thank the following for permission to
reproduce or adapt copyright material:
Dr Francine Patterson and the Gorilla Foundation,
California; Samuel French Ltd for the extract on page 21
from *Aladdin* by John Morley; the author, Giles Brandreth
for a song from his book *I Scream for Ice Cream* on page
22; Macdonald & Co for an extract based on material from
The Time Capsule by Anthony Montcrieff; World Wildlife
Fund; Times Newspapers Ltd for the article on page 55
(adapted from a © T.N.L. article, Sunday Times 2/1/80);
Routledge & Kegan Paul Ltd for adapted extracts from Pile:
Book of Heroic Failures on pages 58, 64 and 89; Sir Robert
Sainsbury and the Sainsbury Centre for Visual Arts; Tom
and Mary Anne Evans for extracts from *Guitars* (Oxford
University Press, paperback forthcoming); Faber & Faber
for the adapted extract and illustration on page 92 from
Gwen Raverat: *Period Piece*.

We should like to thank the following for permission to use
the photographs:
Barratt Developments PLC for page 94; BBC for page 27
(centre); British Tourist Authority for pages 24/25, 44
(inset); Camera Press for page 52 (right); Daily Telegraph
Colour Library for pages 20 (left), 22, 49 (left); Design
Council for pages 12/13; Edimedia, Paris for page 91;
Elisabeth Photo Library for pages 43, 55, 61 (top), 63
(inset), 78; Robert Estall for page 24 (top); Tom Evans for
pages 86, 87, 88; Foster Associates for pages 74, 75; Good
Housekeeping/Anthony Crickmay for page 48; The Gorilla
Foundation/Dr Ronald H. Cohn for pages 6/7 (centre), 8, 9;
John Hillelson Agency/Peter Marlow/SYGMA for pages
33, 34; Alan Hutchison Library for pages 52 (left), 68, 69;
Image Bank for page 54; Irish Tourist Board for pages 49
(top, centre), 61 (bottom); Maier Media Japan for page 66
(left); Manders and Mitchenson Theatre Collection for
pages 18 (right), 19, 20 (right); Mansell Collection for pages
18 (left), 51 (top), 90; Musée du Jeu de Paume, Paris for
page 92 (left); Novosti for pages 66/67 (centre), 66 (bottom);
The Observer for page 14; David Redfern Photography for
pages 27 (bottom), 85 (bottom); Sainsbury Centre for pages
72, 73; Spectrum for pages 36 (top), 36/37 (bottom), 39, 45
(left), 63, 85 (top); Sunday Times/Ian Wright for page 16;
Syndication International for page 92/93 (centre); John
Topham Picture Library for page 60; Trinity College,
Dublin for page 49 (bottom); TV Times for page 45 (right);
Wallace Collection for page 84; Darryl Williams for pages 7,
10, 26 (top), 27 (top), 28, 50 (top), 62 (top).

The cover photograph is by Laurie Lewis/Radio 3
Magazine.

The illustrations are by Oxford Illustrators, and by Roy
Castle/Daily Express (page 44), John Fraser (page 54),
David Parkin (pages 46, 57, 78/79, 80/81), Mike Vaughan
(pages 30, 62), World Wildlife Fund (page 37).

We have been unable to trace the copyright owner of the
picture on page 51 (bottom) and would be grateful for any
information enabling us to do so.